BERT JONES
AND THE BATTLING COLTS

Bert Jones
and
the Battling Colts

Larry Fox

Introduction by John Unitas

ILLUSTRATED

DODD, MEAD & COMPANY
NEW YORK

1 2 3 4 5 6 7 8 9 10

Library of Congress Cataloging in Publication Data

Fox, Larry.
    Bert Jones and the battling Colts.

    1. Jones, Bert, 1951-   2. Football players—
United States—Biography. 3. Baltimore. Football
club (National League) I. Title.
GV939.J62F69   796.33'2'0924 [B]   77-10112
ISBN 0-396-07503-7

To Weeb Ewbank

Acknowledgments

——

Thanks are due all the people who shared their files and their memories with me, including Bert Jones and his teammates Roger Carr, Glenn Doughty, John Dutton, George Kunz, Lydell Mitchell, and Stan White; John Unitas; Ernie Accorsi, Marge Blatt, Barry Jones, and Wilt Browning of the Colts' front office; Paul Manasseh of Louisiana State University; Ted Marchibroda; Pete McCulley; Joe Thomas; Nate Wallack of the Cleveland Browns; Don Weiss and Joe Browne of the NFL; and John Free of the New York Jets, whose late father, Elmer Free, helped secure the beachhead for pro football in Baltimore.

Contents

——

Introduction

—

By JOHN UNITAS

I can still remember the first time I saw Bert Jones play football on television for Louisiana State. The first thing I thought to myself was, "Here's the guy the Balitmore Colts should draft; here's the guy any team looking for a quarterback should draft."

I simply saw that he was fundamentally sound. He didn't run around too much, he'd just get back and sit in that pocket and when he threw the ball he'd give it that good strong arm that you look for. He had the arm, the height, and the quicknesses. I never worry whether a kid's got speed as long as the quicknesses are there. A strong arm and a thirst for knowledge, that's what I look for in a quarterback.

When I watched him then, I was impressed with the way he handled himself, his movements from behind the center, going back, setting up, throwing the football, spotting his receivers. Coaches can tell you the way to do these things and if you pick it up, fine, but they can't really "coach" it.

Right now Bert has by far the best arm in the game. Any

coach in his right mind would give his right arm to build a franchise around him.

I understand from talking to the Colts' people that Bert is quite coachable. He has to be or he wouldn't have come as far as he has this quickly. So you know he has that thirst for knowledge.

He comes into my restaurant here every now and then, usually in the evening after he has picked up some film at the Colts' office. He'll have a few beers, or maybe dinner with me and my wife and son. That's how I've gotten to know him and know that he's fine people. Folks watch us and think we're talking a lot of Xs and Os, but usually it's just, "How ya' feeling? How's your dad? Good luck in the next game" and a lot of hunting and fishing. I wouldn't talk technical football with him unless he brought it up, but we do discuss personnel sometimes and who we're going to be playing on Sunday and what they like to do. It's nothing real deep, but I find we think along the same lines.

One thing I've noticed, Baltimore's offense with Ted Marchibroda is basically similar to what he put in when he was in Washington. Both teams like to run the football more than throw it. Oh, they'll sit back and throw when they have to, but I think they prefer to run it.

Me, I would put the ball up in the air 85 percent of the time and let the running backs just fill in. That's what your strength should be with a good young kid like Bert with his arm and fine outside receivers. Great running backs can run up and down the field all day long between the twenties and never get anywhere.

These are my personal feelings. You've got the quarterback, you should do everything you possibly can to use his abilities. Why run the ball for three, four yards when you can throw it and pick up twenty or twenty-five—or sixty?

Yes, that's the way I felt when I was playing. The running game to me was just something you threw in to fill in the time.

I don't know what Bert's priorities are as far as his future life back home goes, but I think he may be missing something by not spending more time here in the off-season.

Baltimore to me is a town that gave me an opportunity, an opportunity to know the people, to know the town, and to become acquainted not just with the other football players. To know the people of Baltimore to me was a great asset.

All our players seemed to put more effort into getting around town than they do these days. We associated with the people, we had dinner with them and we partied with them, and that's why the fans were able to relate so well to us. It gave you a very warm feeling to know all those people, many of them your friends, were pulling for you. And I know it upset a lot of teams when they came into town and knew they would have to play in that outdoor insane asylum of ours.

Playing for the Colts was a great opportunity for me. We were just starting to build one of the greatest teams of all time when I came here and we had great players like the Donovans, the Pellingtons, and the Marchettis and receivers like Mutscheller, Berry, and Lenny Moore. Then George Shaw got injured and the opportunity was there. It was a matter of whether I took it by the horns or let it pass me by.

The highlight of my career? I played so many good ball games and played some ball games we probably didn't deserve to win and some we lost that we deserved to win, that to me the greatest highlight was just getting the opportunity to play professional football. A lot of people go through their lifetime and never get the opportunity to do what they want to do, but professional football was what I wanted to do.

I know Bert feels the same way about professional football and I know that by the time his career is over he will have many wonderful memories of many great games of his own.

BERT JONES
AND THE BATTLING COLTS

1
The Franchise

——

"If you think it's the coaching, then I'm resigning. We can't go on like this any more."

The slightly built, dark-eyed man who had been standing off to one side spoke quietly. But his brief statement echoed through the crowded room like the warning blast from a policeman's service revolver.

It took only a second or two for head coach Ted Marchibroda's words to sink in.

His Baltimore Colts had just lost their fourth straight exhibition game, 24-9, to the Lions in Detroit's suburban Pontiac Stadium. They had not played well and the 1976 season was opening only a week later.

In the trainer's room, linebacker Tom MacLeod was being given preliminary treatment for a torn Achilles tendon that would finish him for the season and possibly jeopardize his professional career. On another table, defensive tackle Joe Ehrmann was convulsing after a severe concussion. There was fear for his life.

Out in the main locker area, the Colts' unpredictable owner, Bob Irsay, was emotionally berating his beaten players.

Red-faced and perspiring, whether from the heat, anger, or other stimulus, Irsay had stormed into the visitors' clubhouse only minutes after the players clomped in off the field. He ordered out all except actual playing and coaching personnel, but allowed three of his own cronies to remain.

Then, insensitive to Ehrmann writhing in a coma in the next room, he proceeded to give the players a loud and brutal tongue-lashing.

"You guys think you can just turn it on when the season starts, but you can't," he yelled.

He looked around the room and singled out individual players, most of whom he didn't know well enough to call by name when they met under other circumstances. He ripped Don McCauley, who had been a capable running back for the Colts for five seasons, and he turned on Lydell Mitchell, a halfback who was probably the team's best all-around yardage-producer. "When are you going to start playing?" he asked sarcastically of Baltimore's proud 1,000-yard ground-gainer.

One of the reserve defensive backs, Ray Oldham, offered what seemed like a tentative demurrer to Irsay's tirade and he was ordered to apologize and stand facing his locker like a small boy put in a corner.

When he finished with the players, Irsay directed his fire at the coaching staff, head man Marchibroda and his six aides. "You guys haven't been doing your job, either," he sneered. He noted that the St. Louis Cardinals had ten assistant coaches. "Maybe we should get you some help."

At this point, Marchibroda spoke up. This embarrassment had gone far enough. This was not the first time Irsay had made a spectacle of himself in the locker room after a losing game. But it was the first time he had questioned his coach's competence. If he accepted the slur, Marchibroda would lose the respect of his players.

Virtually without thinking, Marchibroda blurted out his resignation.

When the players realized what he had done, they reacted like frightened children about to be orphaned.

"No, no, no!" they yelled and en masse surrounded their diminutive coach, hugging him, clutching at him as if to physically prevent his leaving.

As most of the players rallied to their coach, others tried to talk to Irsay, to make him realize what he had done.

One of these was Raymond Chester, the tall, imposing tight end. He reasoned with the owner, but Irsay, whose soft, pudgy appearance belies his tough upbringing, misread his intentions. Irsay knew he had triggered a storm of hostility among the players, but he wasn't the kind of guy to back down, either. "You don't scare me," the fifty-five-year-old industrialist and former Marine shouted at Chester. "I've been in fights before."

Chester shrugged and turned away.

Irsay asked George Kunz, the stolid offensive tackle and team leader, what had gone wrong "out there" that night. Kunz didn't know. Because of an injury, he hadn't even played in the game. Later Kunz left the room. More than a year later he would still find it upsetting to think about that traumatic scene in Pontiac, Michigan.

As the Colts milled about in the chaotic dressing room, cursing and discussing different courses of action up to and including armed revolt, Bert Jones, the star quarterback, may have started plotting his course.

Even then, he was the only person in the room, including Irsay and his executives, who kept his poise. Quietly he stepped outside to the waiting reporters. "Nothing personal," he told them, "but we've had a few traumatic experiences in here and we'd like you to remain outside."

Since Bert had always been a cooperative friend, the reporters accepted his request. Most thought he was referring to Ehrmann's severe and frightening injury. It wasn't until much later that evening that the full story began to leak out.

Jones had been with the Colts for three seasons and the year before he had emerged as a solid quarterback and team leader on the field. With Jones leading the way, the Colts won their last nine games to gain a spot in the play-offs for the first time in five years.

But he was a quiet youngster and there were many who doubted whether he could ever be a strong force in the locker room, on the airplane, even in the local pubs where so much of the team unity essential to success is forged.

Soon these doubters would get their answer as Bert Jones surveyed the riotous scene.

The erstwhile boy quarterback realized that a man would have to take charge and that he, the most irreplaceable player on the team, would have to fill that role. For the last year or so they had been calling him The Franchise in Baltimore. Even his teammates agreed he was the foundation stone of the team.

Now he would have to act to save the franchise in another sense because, as he knew all too well the Baltimore Colts were going to open their season in just one week—and their coach had quit!

Less than two months earlier, the Colts had been sitting atop the football world as they reported to their training camp at Goucher College in suburban Baltimore.

They were a bright young team on the improve. In 1974 they had showed the bottom line of despair resulting from years of turmoil that included five head coaches in three seasons, a 2-12 record. But only a year later, with Ted Marchibroda installed as head coach, they had turned it all around for a 10-4 record and spot in the play-offs.

Now they were a happy team that would only get better.

The players, mostly the same age, liked each other and rejoiced together as they escaped from the frustrating morass of defeat. Almost all had played on winning teams in college and they were willing to make any sacrifice to keep from sliding back into the bog that claimed the also-rans.

The key player in this revival was Bert Jones. His 1975 improvement had been spectacular. He had worked closely with the new coach, a former pro quarterback himself, to gain his first real understanding of the mysteries of football. This was all he needed to become the complete quarterback. Expert observers agreed unanimously that he was one of the best prospects they had ever seen. He had the strongest arm of any young quarterback in the game and he could run, too, when necessary.

Given their choice of any quarterback in the National Football League, every one of them would have chosen Bert Jones to be The Franchise in his town.

Like most of the young Colts, Bert had been eagerly looking forward to the 1976 season.

"Anticipation with confidence, that's the best way to sum it up," he said. "Everybody goes into a season enthusiastic and anticipating a winning season and going to the play-offs, but it's not necessarily a realistic goal. You can't always figure on going from the cellar to the penthouse. But when you come back after a winning season, you figure you will do it. I was working out in anticipation of having another winning season and going to the Super Bowl. It was a tangible and realistic goal."

The rest of the young Colts and their coaches felt the same way. They couldn't wait for the new season to start.

Yet, something had happened to destroy this aura of good feeling. What had gone wrong?

When they had time to sit back and analyze the situation, most of the Colts realized that Irsay was not the real problem, even if his irrational behavior at football games had triggered the crisis. He had done it before, two years earlier, when he instigated a scene on the sidelines that led him to fire another head coach, Howard Schnellenberger.

The real problem existed between Marchibroda and Joe Thomas, the strong-willed general manager of the Colts and the man who had engineered the deal that enabled Irsay to become the owner in the first place.

Thomas was one of the finest judges of football talent in America and in that capacity had been responsible for the Colts' comeback from oblivion. But he also felt his expertise ranged over all areas of the game and so he liked to impose his judgment on all his subordinates. This included head coaches.

During the 1975 season, he and Marchibroda had worked well together.

Success soured the marriage.

Why? There are two sides, naturally, with elements of justice in both.

Most of the evidence supports Marchibroda.

When the Colts made the play-offs, he was acclaimed throughout the land as Coach of the Year by virtually every newspaper, wire service, and booster club that had the money to buy a trophy. Colt players were lavish in their praise for the job Ted had done in making them winners. None was more outspoken than Bert Jones, the quarterback Thomas had moved heaven and earth to be able to draft.

All this acclaim for Marchibroda rankled Thomas. He had built champions as personnel director in Minnesota and then with the Dolphins in Miami. In each case, though, a strong coach—Bud Grant and Don Shula—had come in at the last minute and reaped all the credit. Now it was happening again.

Although Thomas was named NFL Executive of the Year by the few organizations that awarded such an honor, Marchibroda was beating his boss in the accolade derby at least 10 to 1. Thomas fumed as story after story appeared in the Baltimore press to chronicle another honor for his coach. Thomas even called local sports writers who covered the Colts to complain about the imbalance. "What's the matter, am I dead?" he demanded.

During the off-season, Thomas made some changes in club personnel among those who assisted the coaching staff, apparently overruling or ignoring Marchibroda on some of these decisions. There are reports that he occasionally called Ted to solicit his opinions on these moves, then sarcastically spurned them. It was as if he was using these occasions to demonstrate who was boss.

Then he began tampering with the playing squad. Mike Curtis for some years had been an outstanding linebacker for the Colts. He also had been an outspoken critic of Thomas, dating back to the year when the new general manager was discarding many of Curtis's old teammates.

True, Curtis had been demoted from the starting lineup the season before and he was coming off knee surgery at the relatively advanced age of thirty-two, but he still deserved more than being placed on the expansion list to be sent to the new Seattle franchise. The expansion draft is probably the most demeaning way a player can be discharged.

The Colts got no players or draft help in return and the man who was supposed to replace Curtis, Jim Cheyunski, was himself still limping after serious knee surgery.

Veteran Colts felt Thomas was "getting even" with Curtis for past indiscretions. "He's the kind of guy who will carry a grudge," they grumbled.

Many also felt Thomas had done this "to show Marchibroda who's boss," because the coach had not been consulted on the decision.

This apparently was also the case when Thomas traded backup quarterback Marty Domres to San Francisco during training camp. Domres was making about $100,000 a year, but he was a proven professional, a very rare breed in a critical position.

The Colts thus found themselves going into a championship season with only Bert Jones, a running quarterback and thus susceptible to injury, and an unknown named Bill Troup whom they had looked at and discarded once before.

Quarterback is the most important single position on a football team. The comparable spot on defense is middle linebacker, where Jim Cheyunski stood alone on his suspect knees.

Domres was dealt off for cash and a 1978 fifth-round draft choice. Experienced quarterbacks usually go much higher and Thomas had given up a player and a first-round draft pick to get him only four years earlier.

With no bodies coming in return, players wondered if Thomas wasn't merely saving a couple of big salaries or engaging in a whim when he gave Curtis and Domres away.

The general manager, however, made some pretty cogent points in his own defense.

He noted bitingly that it was Marchibroda who had demoted Curtis the season before and who had suggested that the veteran go ahead and have his knee operated on just to get him out of his hair. Thomas also insisted that during the 1976 preseason, Marchibroda had as much as declared Domres expendable by announcing that Troup was his second-string quarterback. And nobody doubted that the Colts would have to win or lose with Jones no matter who was number two.

Thomas also pointed out that Marchibroda had been well aware of the lines of authority when he came to Baltimore, that he had been so glad to get a head coaching job after fourteen years as an NFL assistant that he was willing to accept any conditions. Thomas said his contract with Irsay gave him the final word on running the club and Marchibroda's deal conformed to these ground rules.

The GM hinted darkly that Marchibroda had been heeding outside advice in plotting his rebellion and that perhaps this direction had come from George Allen, Ted's Machiavellian old boss in Washington. Allen was a coach who had full control over his operation with the Redskins and Marchibroda may have been seeking to create similar autonomy.

Thomas felt it was no coincidence that Marchibroda found a reason to "resign" only one week before the season opener when he would have the strongest bargaining position.

"He knew the conditions when he came here. It was all spelled out in his contract," Thomas charges.

Marchibroda will not discuss the specifics of his grievances against the general manager, but he counters, "There were things he made me do in 1976 that he did not make me do in '75, mainly about who to play and who to keep. He simply changed the ground rules."

What Thomas could never accept was the fact that the general manager's job is by nature an anonymous role, and that's not always bad. What's wrong with dropping into the background when the team is winning? Winning is the whole idea, isn't it? Besides, when the team starts to lose, that makes it easier to jettison the coach. The general manager almost never gets discharged unless he makes himself a visible target.

Too, winning increases a coach's stature. He gets the players on his side and the public as well. The GM who will not bend in these circumstances will lose.

Despite the friction between Thomas and Marchibroda, the Colts started off well by winning their first two pre-season games.

But then they began to lose. Marchibroda said he didn't place much importance on the exhibition games, but Irsay did and so did Thomas because he saw some things he didn't like. Outside observers agreed. The Colts were getting sloppy. They were not playing well.

They lost in Chicago, which hurt because this was Irsay's hometown, and then came defeats against New Orleans and Atlanta, two more weak teams. Irsay chewed out the squad after one of these losses and Thomas gave the assistant coaches a dressing down after another.

When the Colts moved into Detroit for a Thursday night game to kick off the Labor Day weekend, even the players knew they had better do well. The coaches were beginning to show signs of strain and pressure from above.

Bert Jones, so close to Marchibroda—although he will not identify the source of his information—was about the only player who knew the whole story. He just hoped the Colts and Marchibroda could ride things out. He knew Baltimore had the material to be a contender again and, although the team had not been playing that well in preseason, he also knew Marchibroda had been holding back. They went into many of the exhibitions without even a formal game plan. Why tip off the opposition to their full repertoire?

To Marchibroda, the entire training camp and exhibition slate was merely a device to prepare for the official league opener in New England on September 12.

When things calmed down somewhat after Marchibroda's

abrupt resignation, he stepped into the training room to check on Joe Ehrmann's condition. The big tackle would be hospitalized in Detroit overnight for observation. Marchibroda then told his assistant coaches what had happened and next called his wife, Henrietta. "Be prepared for the worst," he told her cryptically. She knew he could not talk freely from the open phone, but she knew what to expect. More than anyone, she had been aware of the growing frustrations under which her husband had labored the last several months.

Ted then showered, dressed, and went out to the team bus. He would return to Baltimore with his team. Thomas, who had stood silently in the background without making any effort to halt Irsay's tirade, had made a previous social engagement and remained in Detroit. Many believed that Thomas, a former coach, had provided the background data for Irsay's attack. The team owner departed for Milwaukee to enjoy the holiday weekend on his seventy-two-foot yacht, the "Mighty I."

The trip back to Baltimore, not surprisingly, was a grim one. On the bus to the airport, Irsay's sixteen-year-old son, Jimmy, who had been working in training camp as a ball boy, tearfully apologized to Marchibroda for his father's attack. "Don't worry, son, you have nothing to apologize for. Your father is a good man," said Marchibroda, himself the father of four.

Marchibroda explained his apparently hasty decision to quit this way:

"In essence, it had been boiling within me for seven, eight months. I thought we [meaning Thomas] had an excellent relationship in '75 that we didn't have in the off-season before '76. It just wasn't the same.

"Finally a reference was made about coaching and I just

felt that was it. The thing is you must have command of your situation and if I accepted this, then I've lost that command. That's it in a nutshell. If that's the way they want it, then get somebody who will do it that way."

By resigning, Marchibroda knew he was walking out on the last two years of his contract and would not be paid. But he had to figure he could easily get another job on the basis of his 1975 Coach of the Year performance. However, if he remained after being demeaned by his owner and general manager the team's performance was bound to suffer, his winning season would be dismissed as a fluke, and his fragile reputation would be ruined. "If I don't resign, I'm dead," he said. "We're going downhill and how am I going to pull 'em out?"

The players understood. "When Irsay had something to say about the assistant coaches, well, that's when Ted blew up because when you're talking about his coaches, you're talking about his family. He had to stand up to be counted," one said.

Meanwhile, Irsay tried to salvage the situation. He denied reports that Marchibroda had been discharged. He issued a statement that explained, "I was telling the team in the locker room that there must be a change, whether it be coaches, players, general manager, secretary, or whatever. I wanted to give Ted a vote of confidence . . . but the players never let me finish. They gave Ted a vote of confidence and that's okay, too. . . . Anyone making more of it than that looks like a fool."

But at this point it was the owner who was wearing the clown suit. He had a potential play-off team and nobody to coach it for the opening game. He soon might not have any players, either.

It was well past midnight when the Colts returned to

Baltimore, and the situation remained somewhat in flux. There had been a lot of yelling, but not too many people were certain just what had been said. Thomas was sure it would all blow over.

The next morning Marchibroda called the general manager in Detroit. "Hey, why bring me into this?" Thomas demanded. Marchibroda said he felt all along the real problem was between them and they should sit down together with Irsay and thrash it out, if possible.

Marchibroda called Irsay and a meeting was scheduled for the three men at the Milwaukee Yacht Club on Sunday.

The meeting was as stormy as anything that had ever blown in off Lake Michigan. It lasted close to six hours and there have been reports, never confirmed, that Thomas and Marchibroda almost came to blows.

Marchibroda spelled out all his grievances and he had a long list of them. Thomas countered with his own arguments and, eventually, the decision was referred to Irsay for judgment.

In essence, Marchibroda wanted greater control of his personnel and closer communication from Thomas. He conceded that he did not need to get involved in the college draft. Thomas pointed out that the chain of command had been spelled out contractually for both himself and the coach. He threw up Ted's own earlier actions on both Curtis and Domres. He noted that he had done pretty well putting together a team for Irsay his way and had made money for his owner besides. Even Irsay, a former college player, could see how poorly the team had been performing lately.

He may even have raised the issue of Marchibroda's alleged treachery in making threats and demands this close to the opener.

Irsay sided with his general manager. He ruled there

would be no changes in procedure. He later classified Marchibroda's complaints about Thomas as "mini-stuff" that seemed to revolve about how often the two men had lunch together.

"If that's your decision, that's it," Marchibroda responded. He got up, walked out and called himself a cab for the airport. En route back to Baltimore he composed a formal statement of resignation. He knew reporters would be awaiting his arrival at St. Mary's Seminary College, the Colts' temporary training base.

Following the informal press conference, he met with his assistant coaches. "I've resigned and that's it," he declared, and two of his personally chosen aides, defensive coordinator Maxie Baughan and offensive line coach Whitey Dovell, said they would quit with him. Many of the players then showed up for a tearful farewell and Mrs. Marchibroda drove Ted back to their home in Falls Church, Virginia, a Washington suburb.

The outcome of the Milwaukee meeting clearly disappointed the players. They had met on Friday, the day after their return from Detroit. Thomas, who had hurriedly flown back to Baltimore, was there. He told the players about the upcoming meeting in Milwaukee on Sunday. The squad deferred action but made no secret of its feelings.

Jones was the spokesman. "It's your ball of wax," he told Thomas. "We want Ted back so we can be a team again. We're giving it to you and we trust you to make the right decision."

There was no question what they felt the right decision would be.

Thomas, meanwhile, was outraged by the way he felt Marchibroda had maneuvered him into this awkward position. His first instinct was to let his coach walk away. If there had been one more week before the opener, he has said unequivocally that he would have done so without hesitation. In retrospect, he feels today that he should have.

Thomas still felt he had two alternatives to asking Marchibroda back. He could take over the coaching reins himself, as he had done two years earlier when Schnellenberger was fired, or he could offer the job to Marchibroda's highly regarded defensive chief, Maxie Baughan. Baughan was loyal to Marchibroda but the temptation of a head coaching job in the NFL might overcome this, especially if he could be persuaded that his friend was finished in Baltimore anyway. Many assistant coaches toil for years, often in vain, for such an opportunity.

His friends persuaded Thomas to discard any thoughts of coaching himself. It would be a disaster to try to follow the popular Marchibroda, especially when the players thought he had played a major role in precipitating the resignation. They would be openly hostile—those that remained, that is.

After the emotional Sunday night meeting with Marchibroda at which the coach's resignation seemed firm, Jones knew what course he had to take. He would move overtly to force Marchibroda's reinstatement.

At 2:00 A.M. he called a friend in the league office at home to ask him to put him in contact with Commissioner Pete Rozelle. "After all, he's the player's commissioner, too," Bert pointed out. Rozelle was spending the Labor Day weekend with friends on Long Island. He and Bert finally spoke by telephone the next afternoon, at which time the quarterback asked Rozelle to use his good offices to talk some sense to Irsay and Thomas to prevent an entire franchise from going down the drain.

Bert, meanwhile, had also been in regular contact with his father, Dub, a former NFL star, in Ruston, Louisiana.

He felt he knew what he had to do, but he wanted his judgment confirmed by a more mature advisor. He also conferred with his brother, Bill, an attorney in Houston. He had to make certain that any actions taken by Colt players would be on firm legal ground. After all, they were under contract to play the season.

Dub's advice to his boy was simple and succinct: "Call a spade a spade and a club a club and get things done. You have everything to win and nothing to lose."

Bert resolved anew to play an individual role in the crisis. There were two aspects to this decision.

In their earlier meetings, many of the Colts had talked angrily about boycotts of practice or even of the opening game that Sunday. Bert realized a lot of this was just talk, that most of the players could not afford to carry out these threats. They had families and mortgage payments and other obligations. He had seen them cave in during the 1974 Players' Association strike when they had legal sanction to walk out. This would be a wildcat strike in breach of contract with more than just financial risk. Fringe players could not afford to chance the enmity of management or they would be cut or traded at the first excuse.

Bert, though, could safely make a stand. He knew why they called him The Franchise. Without being boastful, he knew the Colts could not afford to get rid of him. And if the situation in Baltimore became intolerable he could force the Colts to trade him. Any team he went to would immediately become competitive and he could play for any team in the league. He also could afford to sit out the entire season if necessary. He could always work with his father back home and he had plenty of his own business projects with which to occupy himself. He was single and without family obligations and well off financially in his own right. At his age, sitting out one season would not be fatal to his career. He had plenty of options.

Bert also knew that any attempt to produce a unified team response was doomed. Some players wanted to strike, some did not, feeling with certain logic that their careers were more important than front office wrangling. The coach they went on strike for today still might cut them tomorrow if a better player became available. Whenever this matter was eventually resolved, the players would remember who had stood up with them for Marchibroda and who had not. The squad could have been irretrievably divided.

To salvage the integrity of the team and to protect his less secure teammates, Bert would make his stand as a majority of one.

"I figured I didn't have anything to lose, so I would call the shots—or my shots—because if anyone else had tried to do it, it might have been detrimental to their careers, whereas it couldn't have been to mine because I know I can play somewhere," Bert explained. "You can't ask players to strike if they have a wife or children or payments on a house, so I took it on myself, and the team agreed, to make the statements to the press about our feelings.

"The worst thing that could have happened to me was for Ted not to come back or the coaching staff not to come back and for me to have to play in Baltimore. If I did nothing, there would have been no season and so I had to do something."

On his own, after going over the text with his brother in Houston, Bert prepared a manifesto in support of Marchibroda.

The Colts' players met again on Monday morning. The session opened with a flurry of disagreement about which of several courses to take. Some wanted an immediate boycott of practice. Others suggested that they go ahead and work out, but then strike just before the kickoff against New England to provide maximum embarrassment to the Colts.

After enough of this, Bert got to his feet. He said he was taking over and explained why. His teammates agreed Bert's way would be most effective. He then read the statement. Many teammates volunteered to add their signatures, but Jones declined their offers.

"It was his statement. We didn't approve it, we didn't contribute to it. Our role was to support him," George Kunz explained.

So Bert Jones, once the shy, "yes-sir, no-sir" quarterback, walked out to meet the press and read his statement:

"Every player on this team will tell you that Ted Marchibroda is the man responsible for the success of this team and not the front office. You can put lumber on a lot, but it does not make a house and Ted Marchibroda made this pile of lumber a house.

"Yesterday Robert Irsay and Joe Thomas forced Ted Marchibroda to resign. They were severely wrong in this. It is tremendously unfair to Ted, this town and the team.

"Ted's resignation was forced just because he asked the ordinary powers given to any head coach in the National Football League. He only wanted to select, control and direct his players to be a team. He also asked that Irsay and Thomas respect the ordinary rules of personal conduct in their dealings with him and the team.

"Ted is right. He should be allowed to have the decision authority given other NFL coaches. He has already proven his ability and nobody should have to endure the personal abuse that I have seen Irsay and Thomas give him not only last week but throughout the off-season and exhibition season.

"Thomas and Irsay may have completely destroyed this team by forcing Ted Marchibroda out the week of the first league game. I'm not sure if anyone could put our team back together after the arbitrary action of the front office. The only man who could is Ted Marchibroda.

"Ted Marchibroda should be reinstated as head coach. He should be given the powers of any other NFL head coach to select and direct his team."

This was pretty strong stuff, but Jones wasn't finished.

"I held my feelings in as long as Ted held his, but I have a principle to uphold and I would not be true to myself if I didn't do it," he declared.

He said he felt pity for Baltimore fans, who had so loyally supported the team only to see its front office risk disaster just when they were about to be rewarded for their patience. "That's the saddest thing," he said, and he suggested that if there were any boycotts perhaps they should be by the fans at the Colts' next home game.

He then personally lashed out at both Thomas and Irsay.

"Joe is an egomaniac," Bert declared. "He wanted Ted to know who was boss, but he only belittles himself when he does that."

As for Irsay's locker room tirade that had precipitated the crisis, Jones said scornfully, "I'm not sure if it was all himself speaking or if he let whiskey have a chance."

He added, "Mr. Irsay has painted himself into a corner and doesn't know how to get out except to walk over the paint. And I don't think he's man enough to do that. I'm not sure if Mr. Irsay is smart enough to swallow the apple and say, 'What is the right thing to do?' "

Bert then met privately with Thomas for 2½ hours after first advising the general manager that he had just said some pretty harsh things about him only moments before.

What threats Jones made at this meeting are not entirely clear. Some of his teammates claim that Bert already had made airline reservations back to Louisiana and was ready to get on a plane immediately if Marchibroda was not reinstated. There were even rumors that he had already left.

Bert, though, strongly indicates that while he might have played out the season under whoever was named, he would not have returned the following year. He would have insisted on being traded.

"I told Joe there was nothing left to do but to bring Ted back or he would have lost the season and maybe his football team. Everybody would have been all guns to get out of there by whatever means of transportation they had after the season," Bert said.

Some of the Colts felt even more strongly.

Stan White, the linebacker, says he called his wife and warned her to be ready to "look for a job because I might not be playing this year."

The young veterans who could finally see daylight after years of tumultuous losing were the most upset.

"I wouldn't have played or I would have played someplace else, but there was no way I was going through all that again," White said. "I had seen enough changes in my career, so I was just going to go to law school."

Lydell Mitchell, who had spoken out that morning in support of Jones and strong action to bring Marchibroda back, said flatly, "I won't play." Remember, he had been personally singled out by Irsay in the locker room in front of his teammates.

"I would have asked to be traded," says John Dutton, the defensive tackle. "If Joe Thomas had taken over again or if he had brought in another coach to be a puppet it would have been another 2-12 like my rookie year and I couldn't have gone through that again."

"I was tired of all the chaos, the constant turmoil," says offensive end Glenn Doughty. "We come off a 2-12 season and get into the play-offs and then everything is disrupted because of a nothing game. If we didn't get Ted back, I was going to split."

Other Colts, however, were not so certain. "I was just going to hang in there and do my job, ride it out," says one of the regulars—and there were others.

"There definitely would have been a split," Stan White says. "There were some guys who did not want to stand behind the coach all the way and some like me that did and others who didn't know what to do."

Thomas, meanwhile, issued a brief statement expressing confidence that the coaching situation soon would be resolved—and then he slipped out of his second-story office at St. Mary's via a fire escape to avoid reporters.

By now it was Monday afternoon and time for the Colts to work out. With no coaches expected, Bert was going to run the offensive drill while safety Bruce Laird directed the defense. But some assistants did show up to conduct their preoccupied players through the usual light Monday loosener. Lydell Mitchell pointedly stood off to one side and watched.

Sometime during this period, Joe Thomas played his last card. He had already ruled himself out as coach and, of course, there was no time or capable people available to even consider importing an outsider. He offered the head job to Maxie Baughan.

The balding defensive specialist, a former linebacker, asked for time and used it to call Marchibroda for advice.

"Max, do whatever you think is right, right for yourself and your family. Don't think about me, don't give any consideration to that," replied Marchibroda, who had waited fourteen long years for his own chance to be a head coach.

Baughan had to ponder only minutes to decide "what was right." He declined the offer and Thomas knew he had been checkmated. The opener was nigh and he did not have a coach. Worse, with Baughan and Dovell resigning, the top assistants for both defense and offense also would be missing. Thomas sucked it up and called Ted Marchibroda late that afternoon. He said there was a possibility Marchibroda would be asked back and for Ted to be expecting a call from Irsay the next day. This call from Thomas, incidentally, was how Marchibroda deduced that Baughan had stood behind him and declined the job.

That night, Thomas persuaded Irsay they had to have Marchibroda back. At 9:30 the next morning, Irsay asked his once and now future coach to return to work. Marchibroda says there was some mention of "full authority" in their conversation. He also asked that another year be added to his contract as a token of good will and Irsay agreed.

But the important thing to Marchibroda was simply that he had been asked to return. After all the controversy of the last few days, this was critical. The coach had to have his authority reaffirmed.

Bert Jones's stature as team leader also was firmly established.

"Bert took us all off the hook and everyone knew it," one teammate said gratefully.

"He came out as the definite team leader," said another.

"When Bert stepped forward like that, he really solidified his leadership," agreed a third.

By noon, Ted Marchibroda was back on the job and his Colts exploded with a profane roar of greeting when he walked in to meet with them again. They were overjoyed to have him back.

Jones, for his part, was too emotionally drained to feel

triumphant, even though that day marked his twenty-fifth birthday. "I had no feeling of 'Yay, I won the war,'" he says. "I just felt good for him so he could return and so we could save the season.

"I like to look at the bright side of things and I think that what happened was an underlying blessing because it reestablished team unity. You know, it takes three mules pulling in the same direction to have a winning football team."

Bert's characterization of Irsay, Thomas, and Marchibroda as the three mules of Baltimore was an inspired metaphor.

The timing of the crisis turned out to be fortuitous for the Colts, mainly because the explosion had come after a Thursday night game. If the Colts had concluded their exhibition season on the usual Saturday night or Sunday afternoon, the four days they lost resolving matters would have been disastrous. As it was, they were able to buckle down on their usual game week schedule. Also, most teams spend the entire preseason with their opening opponent in mind. Thus all preparations for almost two months had been geared for New England.

"We haven't lost any time, we're not behind the eight ball," Marchibroda said on his return.

He greeted his players simply. "Well, we're first-and-ten, men."

That, of course, was easier for him to say than for his players to accept. They all felt like third-and-forty with time running out.

Because of all the turmoil and the strong stand they had taken, they now felt under extreme pressure to perform well in the opener. If they lost after getting their precious coach back, they would have been blamed for allowing themselves to be distracted. They also would have proved Thomas and

Irsay right in their doubts about the Colts' preseason performance.

"We had something to prove," said Kunz, and no Colt felt this more than Bert Jones.

"There was a lot of added pressure to this game on everybody and especially on myself," he says. "I had stuck my neck out on the chopping block and if I didn't perform I'd be in a heap of trouble. I was awful anxious for that game to be over."

Nobody realized Bert's predicament more than Marchibroda.

As they walked out on the field before the opening kickoff, he turned to his young quarterback. "Bert, this will be like starting your first high school game."

"Well, coach, I won that one," Bert replied.

"I know you did," Marchibroda answered and he laughed softly.

Bert Jones just smiled. It was time for him to go to work.

2
"I Can Swing Higher"

—

The resolute young man who walked purposefully out on the field to lead the Baltimore Colts into their first game of the 1976 season was predetermined by the boy and the father—and the grandfather, too.

Bertram Hays Jones was born on September 7, 1951, in Ruston, Louisiana, the fourth child and third son of William A. and Schumpert Jones of that city. Ten weeks later, Bert's daddy, on a business trip in his football persona as Dub Jones of the Cleveland Browns, became only the second man in National Football League history to score six touchdowns in a single game. This was against the Chicago Bears. Ernie Nevers had done it before, Gayle Sayers has done it since. So, as of this writing, three names share this NFL record.

Dub Jones spent ten years in professional football, eight of them with the Browns, and in all eight of those seasons his team won a championship. Later Dub would serve as an assistant coach with the Browns, but he was out of the game when, twenty-three years later, his son joined him in the record book by completing seventeen straight passes against the New York Jets. That's a father–son first in the NFL, but we're getting ahead of ourselves.

While Bert may have had the genes to be a great football player, at first he didn't have the legs. As a child he suffered from rickets and the condition left him pigeon-toed and badly bowlegged. For several years before he started school he had to wear braces. (Oddly, there is another NFL super-star who suffered through the same ordeal as a child, even to the extent of having to wear leg braces. You may recognize him leaping over airport suitcases in those television commercials and gaining over 200 yards a game in the NFL. His name is O. J. Simpson.)

Dub Jones thinks it was this early handicap that lit the competitive fires in his son. From the beginning there was always the struggle to keep up and then to be the leader among playmates and older brothers. Poverty is the greatest common denominator that drives professional athletes to succeed. Sibling rivalry is a close second.

All the Jones boys had natural athletic talent and all of them played ball. But, as Dub recalls, "I could see right off that Bert was something special. He had competitive edge. He didn't play games, he attacked them. Whatever Bert tried, he wouldn't stop until he was the best. Tenacious, that's the word for him."

Whether throwing rocks—"Enough to kill a zillion snakes," Bert joked one day in explaining his strong arm—or high-jumping in a homemade backyard pit, Bert had to be the best.

His mother, a determined, religious woman whose strength grew through the months Dub was away playing ball, didn't always approve. She worried about the zeal Bert brought to all his childhood games.

"Why don't you go out and play on your swings for a while?" she once suggested to her fourth-born.

Within minutes, though, she heard Bert challenging a playmate: "Bet I can swing higher than you can."

But braces and brothers weren't the only forces behind Bert's love for competition. Keeping up with these Joneses took some doing.

Bert's grandfather, for instance, had been a four-year all-America in both baseball and football at Tulane University in New Orleans. He was an ambidextrous pitcher who regaled young Bert with tales of how in college he would pitch one game of a doubleheader right-handed and the second game lefty and win them both. Sitting on his front porch he taught his grandson to throw the knuckle ball with which Bert devastated his Little League opponents.

Yet, good as he was as an athlete, grandpa Hap Barnes turned his back on a chance to make the big leagues in either sport to become a dentist.

Dub Jones, Hap's son-in-law, in a sense followed the same route later in life. Dub was an outstanding though late-developing young athlete. During World War II, as a member of various service programs, he was enrolled for part of his college career at Tulane and part at Louisiana State University. There may have been other factors, but the record shows that when he was at Tulane, the Green Wave beat LSU in football and when he was at LSU, the Bayou Bengals beat Tulane.

Dub then starred as a professional with one of the greatest teams ever assembled in the years when the sport was establishing itself. And later he served his old team as an assistant coach.

Yet, when the Browns changed their policy and said they would require their assistants to reside in Cleveland and make coaching a year-round occupation, Dub demurred. Like his father-in-law, he walked away to return to Ruston, where he has prospered as a real estate developer (one report says he owns over 6,000 acres) and owner of a building supply business. To the outsider, Ruston may not seem like much, some 17,000 residents in what is known as Louisiana's "hill country" that seems to consist of scrubby pines, red clay, and crossroads grocery stores with gas pumps out front. But Ruston numbers among its population some thirty millionaires and thus may be head-for-head the richest little city in the nation.

More than that, Ruston represented a way of life to Dub— and also to Bert, who traditionally flees Baltimore for home while the gun signaling the end of the Colts' final game is still echoing through the stadium.

Dub insists he never pushed his sons into football. Bert agrees.

"My father was the main stimulus for me to play ball, but it was more that he had done it and so I wanted to do it," Bert explains today. "He didn't say, 'Here, son, you go throw a football,' but if I wanted to throw a football, he would catch it. To him, it wouldn't have mattered if his children had played ball or not. Each of us has achieved something and he is proud. He'd say, 'Whatever you do, do it as well as you can and I'll be proud.'

"He used to catch for me all the time and still does, even though now I have a younger brother and a first cousin (Andy Hamilton, briefly with the New Orleans Saints) to work with at home," Bert says. "The thing was, he was always there to lend a helping hand. He's a great fundamentalist and although he never 'coached' me—it was kind of show and tell—his theory of throwing a football is a lot like mine. It has to be a natural motion and you can't coach a natural motion. Actually, most of his coaching for me was through baseball. He would help me out more pitching a baseball than passing a football. His advice was always, 'Throw it hard.'"

These early lessons still show up in Bert's passing style.

Perhaps more than any pro quarterback, he throws the ball "over the top." In his distinctive motion he very much resembles a classic baseball pitcher.

Bert's admiration for his father remains unswerving. They will talk football perhaps two or three times a week by phone during the season and they are frequent partners in business transactions. When Bert and the Colts were in crisis, the first person Bert called was his dad.

"He can still run, too, I guarantee you, for fifty yards," Bert adds admiringly. "He runs pastures hunting quail better than anyone I've ever seen and I still can't keep up with him there. He could catch and he could run. In his prime, I don't think there was a better receiver."

As Bert points out, achievement—not necessarily in sports—was what Dub stressed with his children. "If Bert wanted to play the flute, that was fine with me—as long as he played it better than anyone else," Dub once told Ray Didinger of the *Philadelphia Bulletin*. One of the Jones boys was first in his law school class, another was first in his class in Air Force flight training. A daughter is an accountant. Another son, Ben, was the last cut of the St. Louis Cardinals as a wide receiver a few years ago. They asked him back the following season but he respectfully declined because he was too well established in his new career as an engineer. Young Tom, expected to be an even better athlete than Bert, shocked the entire clan not too long ago when his high school report card showed a B. It was the first time he had failed to make straight As.

"Football is important in our family but it's not the only thing," Bert says. He brags that his whole family "has smarts," but points out modestly that "I'm the black sheep." That's because his college grades settled in the jock-C category. But ol' Bert is catching up. Thanks to his multitude of business interests and real estate investments parlayed out of his football earnings, he is probably close to being another of Ruston's millionaires.

Bert's first touch of the world of pro football came even before he started school. Autumns were spent in Cleveland, where his father was playing ball. His earliest memories are not of the games, which he attended, but of sitting on an equipment trunk in the middle of the Browns' locker room waiting for Dub to shower and get dressed. (Others recall that on the Browns' weekly "family day," usually Saturday when the team engaged in a light workout, young Bert could often be seen wandering into the huddles.)

The Browns of those days were an awesome football aggregation, possibly the most dominant team the game has ever known. All-time greats like Otto Graham, Marion Motley, Mac Speedie, Dante Lavelli, Len Ford, Bill Willis, and Lou Groza illuminated the roster. Dub Jones was pretty good. He made all-pro in 1951. On any other team he might have been a superstar. In this cast he was just one of many able supporting actors. But he has no regrets. There were all the championships, plus the knowledge that he had made a vital contribution in concert with those legendary stars.

As with most championship teams, there was a continuity to the Browns. The same people returned year after year and, because rosters were smaller, the players and their families grew close. While sitting on that trunk as a preschooler, young Bert sensed he was privy to something special. With all those victories, the locker room was almost always a happy place, but more likely the kid was mostly anxious for his daddy to get dressed so they could leave. Perhaps that evening they would be having dinner with Uncle Warnie—the late Warren Lahr, one of Dub's closest friends on the Browns—and his family.

Eventually school commitments intruded on Bert's winters in Cleveland, but already this particular twig had been bent.

"What do you want to be when you grow up?"

Mrs. Bell always asked this question of her first-grade students at Hillcrest Elementary School in Ruston on opening day.

The other boys had responded with the usual litany of the joys of life as a fireman or a policeman.

"I want to be a professional football player," Bert answered when his turn came.

"But what if you can't be a professional football player?"

"Then I don't want to be anything."

Mrs. Bell understood. She also had been Dub Jones's first-grade teacher.

The Jones family eventually grew to include seven children (five boys) domiciled in a rambling white frame house away from the center of town. The house was comfortable, built for living, visitors recall. The front yard was fabulous. By some coincidence, it measured 100 yards long and some 30 yards wide. The length and almost the width of a football field. Goalposts soon sprouted at one end of the yard. Before long the Jones front yard became the meeting place for all the neighborhood boys. Over the years, as the boys improved, the "neighborhood" expanded to include football players from all over northern Louisiana.

Ruston is the site of Louisiana Tech, the school that sent Terry Bradshaw to the pros. It is three miles from Grambling, alma mater of the Rams' James Harris and dozens of other NFL standouts. There were always plenty of quarterbacks, wide receivers, and defensive backs for a full-scale workout to help everybody get in shape before the high school, college, or pro season.

Bert proudly points out that four current NFL quarterbacks—all of whom have taken their teams to the play-offs at one point or another—grew up within 100 miles of each other along the same highway, old U.S. 80, now Interstate 20. They are himself, Harris, who hails from Monroe, Louisiana, and Bradshaw and Buffalo's Joe Ferguson from Shreveport.

Football in this area was as much a way of life as hunting, fishing, and cutting timber for profit.

In junior high, Bert played one football season as a center and then moved to quarterback forevermore. After his sophomore year in high school, he gave up basketball. The next year he gave up baseball.

Bert still feels that when he finished high school he was better in baseball than in football. As a pitcher, thanks in part to his grandfather's knuckle ball, he once threw nine straight Little League no-hitters.

Today he gives two reasons for quitting baseball. The obvious first reason is that he didn't want to risk hurting his arm. But this was not primary in his thinking. Jones always has been one to set his priorities, from that first day in the first grade. "I realized," he said—and remember, this is a high school junior thinking—"that one day I was going to have to make a decision between football and baseball and I didn't want to make that decision a difficult one."

Baseball to Bert was a game. Football was a calling. He did not want to risk the temptation of those baseball scouts with their $100,000 bonuses if that day of decision ever came.

Still, in his senior year, the hyperactive Jones had to come up with something physical to fill up his spring. So he took up the javelin—and won the state championship.

Bert's intimacy with pro football resumed during his high school years. His father by now was an assistant coach with the Browns and he took Bert to training camp for several summers in the tiny college town of Hiram, Ohio.

It wasn't completely a vacation for Bert. That wasn't Dub's way. His children worked for all of their spending money. The lumber yard and construction business provided countless opportunities for the Jones kids and they accepted it as a way of life. "If I wanted a dollar, I never asked for it, I just hauled two-by-fours for two hours to earn it," says Bert, who recalls that he never owned a car of his own until he signed with the Colts. At LSU he shared a pickup truck on campus with his brother and sister.

Bert earned his "vacation" at Hiram—an idyllic college town that was almost deserted when the Browns were there because school was out—by working as a ball boy.

Ball boy. A euphemism. The ball boy is the jack-of-all-dirty-jobs in a football training camp. Pick up towels, pick up jocks, launder socks, shine shoes, haul ice, sweep the floor, be there before the players, stay late. Long hours, hard work—heaven.

Bert's special friend was Bob Nussbaumer, son of another assistant coach. Together they would put on their shorts and Cleveland Browns tee shirts and saunter out to the practice field wearing the same uniform as the injured players. A harmless fantasy that fooled no one, but it was fun to pretend. It was the same feeling during those solitary times when work was done, the players departed, and the two teen-agers splashed around in the whirlpool tubs.

There were other magical moments. Sometimes the boys shagged punts and kickoffs and field goals by the legendary Lou Groza. And, as practice began, Bert often helped warm up the quarterbacks, Frank Ryan and Jim Ninowski.

Bert was a shy and respectful kid, they all remember, blond and somewhat toothy, just growing out of adolescent awkwardness. "Yes, I remember Bert," Frank Ryan recalled recently. "He certainly had the makings, even then. He was very much cut in the mold of his father and even though he was very quiet and gentlemanly, he stood out. He had the same delivery of the ball then that he does now, although he's gotten a lot stronger. That natural delivery of his is something you get early and if you don't have it early, you will have difficulty developing into a great one."

Bert carefully observed the styles of the two experienced professionals. Ninowski occasionally would offer a little tip, but Bert feels he may have patterned himself more after Ryan. "It was one of those 'I see, I try, I do' things," he recalls.

During these years, Dub would explain some of the technical things that were going on whenever his boy asked, but mostly, Bert says, "What I learned was the desire to play."

There was the other side, too, the bitter underside of pro football. The great Browns team of his father's generation was aging. Familiar faces disappeared with each passing summer. "I learned then that pro football was a business; if you don't produce you go," Bert says.

Although his sharpest memories are of the quarterbacks, Bert spent most of his time with equipment manager Morrie Kono and trainer Leo Murphy. They were in charge of the ball boys and they sort of adopted Dub's kid.

Bert made his professional debut as the starting quarterback for Baltimore in the opening game of the 1973 season in Cleveland against the Browns. Leo Murphy and Morrie Kono were among the first to greet him when he came out of the tunnel for pregame warm-ups.

For almost his entire life, Bert Jones had dreamed of playing professional football for the Cleveland Browns. To this day, in fact, he cannot refer to that team in the familiar form. It is one word: *Clevelandbrowns*. Brownies? Never.

"All my life I had dreamed of being a Clevelandbrown," he says. "I had been in that stadium so many times, but always on the other side of the field. Then, when I walked out on the field and saw all the people and players I grew up admiring and all the trainers I had worked for and the ball boys, it was startlingly real—and kind of funny. A bittersweet moment."

The sentiment of that moment when Dub's boy came back to Cleveland Stadium as a budding star in his own right remains as sweet as ever. But Jones was sacked five times and the Colts lost the game, 24–14. Defeat to Bert carries a lingering aftertaste, like sour wine or a cheap cigar.

Dub Jones, who would settle for a flute player only if he was the best, knew how Bert felt the day he came back to Cleveland.

3
Call Them Colts

In a sense, Daddy Dub was the first Jones ever to play for the Colts' franchise, or at least the granddaddy of the Colts' franchise. And as one studies the history of this troubled team, the roots of the tumult of today become clearly visible. Ball clubs, like families, develop self-perpetuating personalities. Owners, coaches, and entire rosters may change but, win or lose, the franchise retains its hereditary stamp. The Colts were to be cursed with controversy.

Only originally they were not Colts. They were Seahawks, Miami Seahawks.

The year was 1946. World War II had just ended and the American public was starved for entertainment, live entertainment. Television had not yet become the force it is today, nailing Americans to their easy chairs. Veterans were back from the war. Their families reunited, their savings accounts heavy, they wanted to go places and have fun. The movie industry thrived. So did the world of sports.

As an example, these years marked the last golden age of minor league baseball before television made the species virtually extinct. Other sports did as well and expansion was the order of the day, not only because the public had the bucks but because the end of the war unleashed a vast stock-pile of manpower. College enrollments overflowed and stu-dents often were domiciled in army surplus Quonset huts. Many of these returnees were athletes, mature athletes, often with families, and eager to turn professional. Many high school stars had enjoyed top competition on service teams and felt they were ready to skip the rah-rah game.

The late Arch Ward, promotion-minded sports editor of the *Chicago Tribune*, thought it was time to start a new circuit to rival the National Football League.

He called his creation the All-America Football Confer-ence and named Jim Crowley, the former Notre Dame star, as its first commissioner. Franchises were awarded to eight teams. Baltimore, considered briefly, was passed over in favor of Miami.

The Seahawks were owned by the late Harvey Hester, a picaresque restaurateur of huge girth and appetite who early on discovered that this was one of the few times in his full life that he had bitten off more than he could digest. The Seahawks opened their first year during the hurricane sea-son, and for their first several Orange Bowl dates crowds were held down by drenching rains. (Perhaps this is why the latter-day Seahawks, Seattle's new expansion team, plays its games in a domed stadium.) When Hester finally got good weather for one of his games, it turned out to be the eve of Yom Kippur, holiest of Jewish holidays. Miami has a large Jewish population. The moon finally shined over Mi-ami, but only to illuminate more empty seats.

Hester, certain he had been cursed by a higher power, at this point surrendered and eventually opened a fine restau-rant in a converted slave cabin outside Atlanta. The Sea-hawks, who won only three of fourteen games, completed the season as wards of the league.

The Jones family link was established during Hester's custodianship. One of the rookie players he signed was a two-way star from Louisiana named Dub Jones. The contract called for $12,500 a year.

"It doesn't sound like much now, but I was the highest paid player on the team," says Dub, who notes that on the day son Bert signed his rookie contract with the Colts, "he picked up more money than I made in my entire career."

Considering his high salary and the Seahawks' financial plight, it was no surprise that Dub was traded by Miami during the season to the Brooklyn Dodgers. The Dodgers, in turn, in 1948 traded Dub to Cleveland. "I played for three teams in my first three years in the league and I began to wonder if there was something wrong with me, but I found a home in Cleveland," Dub says.

When the AAFC folded after the 1949 season, Dub moved with the Browns, who had started using him more and more as a pass receiver, into the established NFL. There he and his Cleveland teammates proved they could win in any company.

Meanwhile, the Seahawks' franchise was moved to Baltimore for the 1947 season when fun-loving Bob Rodenberg, a Washington promoter, put together a syndicate to run the club.

The nickname of Colts was selected through a fan poll as symbolizing Maryland's horsey atmosphere. The name was new, but the team colors of green and silver were retained from the old Seahawks. That way some of last year's jerseys could be saved.

Another color the Colts inherited from Miami was red, as in ink. Rodenberg and his associates lost some $165,000 that first season, plus eleven of fourteen games. One of their two victories (they also played a tie) was against the Dodgers and Dub Jones. Cecil Isbell was coach of these first Colts.

At the close of the season, Rodenberg turned the franchise back to the league. He had suffered enough. Admiral Jonas Ingram, by now the commissioner, was all set to sell the franchise to a group in Dallas, but he first met with Baltimore's mayor, Thomas D'Alesandro. D'Alesandro moved quickly to save the franchise.

The first men he contacted were two minor partners from Baltimore who had been in Rodenberg's Washington-oriented group. They were Charles P. McCormick, head of the spice company that bears his family's name, and Jake Embry, owner of a radio station and a professional basketball team, the Baltimore Bullets. Embry agreed to serve as president as a blue ribbon citizens committee was hastily gathered to back the Colts. They paid the league $25,000 for Rodenberg's assets and were handed the franchise debt-free. According to John Steadman's history of the Colts, Rodenberg would have liked to have been a member of the new group, but nobody asked him. This was to be an all-Baltimore production.

Still, it was Rodenberg in one of his last acts as president who persuaded the Browns to turn over the draft rights to a young LSU quarterback named Y. A. Tittle. The AAFC chipped in with some additional player help, Isbell was retained as head coach and the 1948 Colts posted a 7-7 record.

That was good enough for a first-place tie in the Eastern Division with Buffalo, but the Bills won the play-off, 28-17, on a disputed call at the end for the dubious privilege of losing to Cleveland, 49-7, for the league title.

The Colts once again lost money, almost $50,000, and it took a close vote by the directors to keep the team going into 1949. McCormick at that time promised to personally underwrite future losses with a secret "blank check" commitment.

The rest of the teams in the conference, though, did not

have such committed owners. They were all set to quit the expensive war, with Cleveland and San Francisco moving into the NFL. The Dons of Los Angeles would merge with that city's NFL team, the Rams. Buffalo interests would merge with the Cleveland Browns to join the older circuit. Similar deals reportedly were available for all the other teams—except Baltimore.

Aware of these backstage machinations, the Colts put on an optimistic face at the league meetings and effectively blocked a merger that would not have included Baltimore. (There would have been serious antitrust implications had the Colts been frozen out.)

Thus stymied, their reluctant partners in the AAFC had to struggle through still another costly season. The Colts paid a price, too. Their record was 1 and 11, Isbell was fired at mid-season with general manager Walter Driskill replacing him, and the franchise lost close to $100,000.

The war between the leagues, by escalating salaries, also was expensive for the NFL. There had to be a merger. The cost was inclusion of Baltimore as a thirteenth team along with the originally scheduled pair of survivors, Cleveland and San Francisco.

The Colts' financial losses do not seem that great today, but that was before inflation had diminished the dollar. In those days this was big money. And yet, if the AAFC had enjoyed the cushion of even a minimal television contract, such as helped launch the American Football League a decade later, it might still be alive today.

Despite the merger, the Colts were far from a substantial operation. Would the directors agree to back the team again? They couldn't count on McCormick's continued largess and so they hesitated.

Into this vacuum of doubt stepped one Abe Watner, a

flamboyant Baltimore trucking magnate who also owned a large cemetery, which he once described as dealing in "underground bungalows."

Watner knew zilch about football, but he enjoyed the limelight and he said he would underwrite the Colts through 1950 if they would name him president. The directors agreed on condition that they could take the team back at season's end by reimbursing Watner for any losses. Watner safely added that if the team made any money during his stewardship, he would give these profits to charity.

One of the ways Watner kept down expenses was by personally handing out sticks of chewing gum to his players one at a time before games rather than allowing them to dip their mitts freely into an open box, the usual practice. (His suggestion that the sticks be cut in half for double the mileage if not the pleasure was ignored, according to Steadman.)

Watner's new coach was Clem Crowe, and the team started out in the red by paying the Washington Redskins the first $50,000 of a $150,000 indemnity for encroaching on their NFL territory.

Unlike the powerful Browns, who won the championship their first season in the NFL, the Colts were overmatched in their new company. They lost all seven exhibition games and their first six in regular season, including a 70-24 disaster to the Los Angeles Rams. The franchise at this point was doomed. Attendance plummeted below even AAFC levels as the Colts staggered home with another 1-11 record.

Instead of going back to the Colts' directors or their 200-odd public stockholders to see what could be done to save the team for Baltimore, Watner voluntarily surrendered during the January league meetings. He returned the franchise to the league and in exchange was paid $50,000 for the team's assets, which presumably went to defray his personal losses. The players were then distributed through the league, at least those anyone wanted.

The other Baltimoreans, who had worked so long and spent so much money in previous years, were enraged at the betrayal. The directors called an emergency meeting and instituted a law suit against both Watner and the NFL. They said their erstwhile president had exceeded his authority by selling the franchise and giving away the players and the league had acted illegally to approve these maneuvers.

The league, however, seemed happy to be rid of the franchise they had only reluctantly included in the merger and a year later passed up an opportunity to restore Baltimore to the NFL. By 1952, the NFL had another team in trouble: the New York Yankees, formed originally in Boston by Ted Collins, wealthy manager of singer Kate Smith. But instead of selling this club to Baltimore interests, they unloaded it to a group of oil tycoons from Dallas.

The move to Texas proved a disaster. After six straight defeats, four of them at home before tens of thousands of empty seats in the huge Cotton Bowl, the owners gave up. Their dreams of instant success had turned into a dry well. The franchise was returned to the league and the Dallas Texans, as they were known, played their remaining games on the road. The squad was domiciled in Hershey, Pennsylvania, and worked out there. Their only victory in twelve games came on Thanksgiving Day in Akron, Ohio, before 3,000 paid fans, 27-23 over the Chicago Bears.

With the collapse of the Texans, the old Colts' ownership pressed their lawsuit. They didn't want their money back, they didn't want damages, and they turned down a cash settlement. They simply wanted another crack at pro football. These people were so dedicated, the Colts' marching band kept practicing for two years even when the city didn't have a team. Baltimore wanted that Dallas franchise.

Bert Bell, commissioner of the NFL, was on a spot with a sick franchise, a lawsuit, and a city that wanted the team. But still he imposed conditions. He told Baltimore interests that if they got a suitable person to become 51 percent owner and sold 15,000 season tickets, they could have the franchise.

The majority owner Bell had in mind was Carroll Rosenbloom, son of a wealthy Baltimore-based clothing manufacturer who had gone on to make a huge fortune of his own by producing work clothes and army fatigue uniforms. Rosenbloom, then forty-three, later invested in railroads, electronics, and the movie industry. He no longer lived in Baltimore but he had business and family ties there. Rosenbloom had played college football at Pennsylvania and his backfield coach was Bell. Later they would be neighbors in Margate, New Jersey.

For some time Rosenbloom resisted Bell's pleas that he take over the Colts. But finally he gave in when the commissioner publicly said that his old halfback was the man he had in mind to bring pro football back to Baltimore.

Even though the ticket campaign took place during the Christmas holidays, Baltimore easily beat Bell's deadline. The 15,000 tickets were sold with some to spare and $300,000 to pay for them was safely in the bank.

The Colts were back in business with the remnants of the Dallas roster. Rosenbloom owned 52 percent of the team with four local partners, whom he eventually would buy out.

There is considerable speculation as to how much money Rosenbloom actually put up to get control of what turned out to be one of the league's most lucrative franchises.

He says the team cost $200,000 and that is not wrong. But

it is not correct, either. At first the league asked merely for a $50,000 down payment but later this was scaled in half. Thus Rosenbloom actually got in merely for a pledge to ante up at most $13,000 of the initial payment.

However—and this was a big however—all the money was already in the bank! Baltimore sources say the $300,000 in advanced sales guaranteed that the team would break even its first year.

Rosenbloom did say he was putting aside a private war chest of over $1 million to cover future operating expenses, but the Colts became such an immediate success that this money was never touched. The $200,000 to buy the team was paid for out of profits, which also could be described as the source of the $1,725,000 Rosenbloom eventually paid to buy out his partners.

Rosenbloom became sole owner in 1964 when he bought out his three remaining partners and even this event is fraught with controversy. The deal was completed only three days before the NFL announced its first national television contract, a development that would have vastly increased the value of the team. CR's old partners charged that Rosenbloom knew about this imminent development when he bought them out at the old rates, and they threatened to sue.

In any event, Rosenbloom's total cash investment was miniscule. Capitalizing on his own business acumen and the fact that he bought in on the eve of pro football's popularity explosion, Rosenbloom made millions on the franchise.

Rosenbloom eventually had the greatest single influence on Baltimore football of any man, including his most famous players, like John Unitas, and his great coaches, like Weeb Ewbank and Don Shula.

Rosenbloom was a fierce competitor with an insatiable need to succeed that undoubtedly was responsible for his good fortune in the business world. On game days he felt the tension even more than his players. He operated the Colts like a benevolent godfather. No aspect of the operation was too small for his attention. He sat in on the college draft and had the final say on top selections and all trades.

He liked to think of the football team as an extension of his family. He involved himself in all areas of his players' lives. He listened to their problems, got them off-season jobs, set them up in business for their days after football.

Buddy Young, who came to Baltimore with the Texans, still remembers the first day of training camp when the new owner actually appeared in the locker room and introduced himself to the players. This was unheard-of then. He also told some of the veterans that he was new to the game and would need their guidance.

He helped make Gino Marchetti, his great defensive end, a millionaire by setting him up in the fast food business.

As Unitas recalls today, "It was always a family-oriented situation. Mr. Rosenbloom was not only concerned about the players, but with their family needs. You never did anything without Mr. Rosenbloom or management knowing about it and if they could be of any help they would. If one of your children was sick and you needed a specialist for a doctor, they got you a specialist for a doctor. You never had to settle for some quack down the street."

As fast as the league outlawed each practice, Rosenbloom thought of new ways to reward his players with extra bonuses. But in all this, of course, he was not being purely altruistic.

Rosenbloom realistically was aware that his players performed better when they were freed from outside distractions and worry. And, too, a player's knowledge that he will be remembered by management when his playing days are over is enough to inspire any athlete to make the little extra sacrifice.

Rosenbloom's finest moment came soon after he took control of the Colts. Baltimore held a "welcome home" dinner for the team at a downtown hotel on the eve of the opener and included among the players were two black stars, Buddy Young and George Taliaferro of the old Dallas Texans.

"Baltimore was still a 'southern' city in those days," Young recalls. "I remember they had an open bar at the party. George and I had brought our wives and several friends but the waiters refused to serve us and so we left. When Carroll found out about what had happened, he and his wife walked out of the party, too. They found out where we had gone and joined us."

Rosenbloom did not back down when it came to breaking Baltimore's color line—and a year later Buddy Young was honored by fans as the Colts' most popular player.

At the suggestion of Bert Bell, Rosenbloom hired Don Kellett as his first general manager and Keith Molesworth as his first coach. He quickly realized Molesworth was unsuitable for the job and almost fired him in training camp. But he held off and spent the 1953 season learning about the game of professional football and hunting for a successor.

The place to look was on the staff of the most successful team in the league, the Cleveland Browns. Blanton Collier, one of Paul Brown's aides, turned him down, but then Rosenbloom offered the post to another Cleveland assistant, Weeb Ewbank. Brown didn't want to lose one of his top aides and his reluctance to let Weeb go created some bitterness between them, but eventually Ewbank took the job with a three-year contract.

Wilbur C. (Weeb) Ewbank was a teacher and an organizer, a stubby little Hoosier who looked as if he belonged behind the counter of a small-town hardware store. Or perhaps lecturing high school students as the principal at a rural consolidated school.

But he knew his football and he knew his football players. "He could take a dozen guys down to his basement, run 'em around the Ping-Pong table and tell you which ones would be pros," a former player, Jimmy Orr, once declared.

The Colts had a few pretty good players when Weeb arrived, fellows like Art Spinney, free-spirited, beer-drinking Art Donovan, aggressive Bill Pellington, and hard-boiled Gino Marchetti, whom Ewbank immediately shifted from offensive tackle to defensive end.

When hired, Ewbank told Rosenbloom it would probably take five years to produce a winner and his first year he added such as Alex Sandusky, Buzz Nutter, Jim Mutscheller, and colorful Don Joyce, who wrestled professionally in the off-season.

The Colts were still only 3-9 in 1954, the same as they had done under Molesworth, but Ewbank was slowly building. And for the next season he had a brilliant draft that included quarterback George Shaw with a bonus pick, fullback Alan (The Horse) Ameche on the first round, center-linebacker Dick Szymanski on the second, halfback L. G. Dupre on the third, and guard George Preas on the fifth.

Another addition that season, chosen as a "future" on the twentieth round the year before, was a slender, bespectacled pass receiver from Southern Methodist University named Raymond Berry. Nobody ever called him Ray and when they first saw him, few would call him a football player, either. He was skinny, weighed less than 180 pounds, and had a bad back. One leg was shorter than the other due to a childhood illness. But he would run patterns by the hour, study films for days on end, and when he didn't have a quarterback to throw him passes, he put his wife to work. That's probably how be invented his "bad pass" drill. By will and intellect Raymond Berry made himself a Hall of Fame pass receiver.

It didn't hurt to have John Unitas to throw to him, either.

The Colts improved to 5-6-1 in 1955 and held at 5-7 the next season, but this marked their turning-point year. All because Weeb Ewbank read his mail. From Pittsburgh came a letter suggesting the Colts look at a local sandlot quarterback named John Unitas. Unitas had been drafted ninth by the Steelers out of the University of Louisville the year before but never got a chance to play in a game. Art Rooney is the owner of the Steelers and his twin sons that year were ball boys in the Pittsburgh camp at St. Bonaventure University in Olean, New York. One day they wrote their father about a rookie who was "the best quarterback in camp but the only people they let him throw to is us and we're not on the team."

They were, of course, referring to Unitas. Walt Kiesling, then coach of the Steelers, didn't share the twins' enthusiasm. He thought Unitas was "too dumb" to be a big league quarterback.

And so he kept Jim Finks and Ted Marchibroda and a guy named Vic Eaton, who also could punt and play defense. Finks later became a successful general manager of the Bears and the Vikings. Marchibroda became a Coach of the Year with the Colts. Maybe they were smarter than Unitas but neither will make the Hall of Fame off his exploits on the field.

Unitas recalls vividly the weekend he was cut. "Marchibroda was off at National Guard camp or something and so I had been playing behind Finks and Vic Eaton but I hadn't got into a single game for even one play that preseason. Now we're playing Detroit in Florida and we're getting whipped real bad and Finks is having a bad night. Marchibroda had just joined us that same day. With two minutes to go, Kiesling looks right at me. So I grab my helmet and I jump up to go into the game and he says, 'Marchibroda.'

"We flew home to Pittsburgh that night and they gave us the weekend off. Sunday night I drove with Finks and Lynn Chadnois to Franklin, Pennsylvania, to pick up Teddy and then we drove on up to Olean. We drove all that way and the next morning Nick Skorich says, 'Take your [play] book, Coach Kiesling wants to talk to you,' and I was cut. They made me drive all the way up there, about 300 miles, and then they gave me ten dollars to take the Greyhound back home. That was what a bus ticket back to Pittsburgh cost— but I hitchhiked to save the ten dollars."

But Unitas was tough. His father had died when he was five and his mother had raised four children scrubbing floors, selling insurance and, finally, as a bookkeeper for the city. A grandmother and an uncle lived with them and today Unitas still remembers sticking cardboard in his shoes and trying to glue on ten-cent replacement soles he had bought at the local hardware store.

After the Steelers cut him he worked on a construction gang, lived with his in-laws, and played semi-pro football for the Bloomfield Rams for six dollars a game. He would be a pro.

Weeb always accused Unitas of sending out that initial letter himself, but he checked it out. He called Frank Camp, John's college coach at Louisville, and he talked with a member of his own scouting staff, Herman Ball, who had been an assistant with the Steelers the year before. Both urged Ewbank to give Unitas a look. After a tryout that spring in a public park, the Colts signed him to a $7,000 contract. The story goes that Unitas was signed for the price of a seventy-five-cent phone call, the supposed toll when Don Kellett called him to come down for that tryout.

Among other newcomers that year were rookie Lenny Moore, one of the most exciting runners the game has ever known, and a veteran defensive lineman claimed on waivers from Los Angeles, Gene (Big Daddy) Lipscomb. Lipscomb had never attended college and even though his private life was tangled, his old teammates were shocked at his sudden death of a drug overdose under mysterious circumstances in 1962.

On the field, as in life, Big Daddy was awesome. He teamed with Donovan at tackle, and with Marchetti and Joyce at the ends, Ewbank had finally put together the defensive line so necessary for any championship team.

He also had the offensive line and the receivers in Berry and Mutscheller and the runners in Ameche and Moore. All that remained was the quarterback.

The season opened with George Shaw as the starter. Shaw was a fine-looking prospect out of Oregon and the Colts figured they could go all the way with him. However, in the fourth game of the season Shaw suffered a fractured kneecap and he was declared out for the season. Unitas had to come in and at first he was terrible. He hadn't played really competitive football in over a year and it showed.

By season's end, though, Unitas had won some big games for the Colts and Ewbank decided the slope-shouldered Pennsylvanian was to be his quarterback.

The biggest game Unitas won in 1956 was the last. The Colts went into their finale against the hated Washington Redskins (fans still remembered that indemnity payment) with a 4-7 record, a three-game losing streak, and Ewbank's job very much in jeopardy.

Rosenbloom had been openly critical of Ewbank most of

the season and there were reports he almost fired him after the fourth game of the schedule, a 58-27 rout at the hands of the Bears. It was an open secret in Baltimore that Weeb would be let go after the season since his original three-year contract was up.

Weeb probably was finished as the game went into the final minutes with the Colts trailing, 17-12. But then Unitas threw one of those Hail Mary passes downfield. The ball deflected off a Redskin defensive back into Mutscheller's hands, and the big end dragged two tacklers the last five yards into the end zone for the decisive touchdown in a 19-17 Colt victory.

Rosenbloom, then as always highly emotional, was overcome with the moment. He told Ewbank he could return with a new three-year contract.

Ewbank and the Colts almost won it all in 1957. The main new recruit was Jim Parker, a massive tackle from Ohio State and the team's number one draft choice. Parker got a rude initiation. He was matched in preseason drills against the veteran Marchetti. One day Ewbank instructed Marchetti to go all out against the rookie, and no matter what Parker tried, the veteran whipped him with a virtuoso performance. "What do I do now?" Parker asked a teammate. "I would suggest you applaud," came the reply from one who appreciated Marchetti's talents.

Fortunately for Parker, he did not have to play against very many Marchettis, and eventually he would join his one-time nemesis (plus Berry, Donovan, and Moore, as of this writing) in the Hall of Fame.

The Colts went into their final two games of 1957 with a one-game lead over Detroit and San Francisco in the NFL's Western Division. (This geographical paradox was a legacy of the Texans.) They were scheduled to play in San Francisco and then remain on the west coast for the season windup in Los Angeles.

The game against the Forty-niners was a tough one. Y. A. Tittle, Frisco's quarterback, was knocked out of action but his substitute, John Brodie, came in to throw the winning touchdown pass in a 17-13 score. The Colts and Ewbank still insist that play should have been called back because the receiver, Hugh McElhanny, had "pushed off" against defensive back Milt Davis. "Hell, he grabbed him by the jersey and spun him around," says Unitas, still indignant today.

But neither the officials nor the game films caught the alleged infraction. The disheartened Colts went on to lose their last game in Los Angeles, 37-21, for a 7-5 record.

The Lions and Forty-niners tied at 8-4 and the Lions won the play-off and went on to beat Cleveland for the NFL title.

Weeb had said it would take five years to produce a winner. He was almost fired after three, almost made it after four, but now in season five he knew his Colts were ready to make a run for it. "This is your year to know and be known," he told his players in training camp.

The Colts won their first six games, survived a mid-season rib injury that idled Unitas for most of three games, and won the NFL's Western Division championship with a 9-3 record.

The Giants, meanwhile, needed to win their last two games to tie Cleveland in the Eastern Conference. They came from behind to beat the Lions, 19-17, and then rallied for a 13-10 victory over the Browns on a forty-nine-yard Pat Summerall field goal. A week later they beat the Browns again, 10-0, to move into the championship round against the rested Colts.

These were two outstanding football teams that lined up in Yankee Stadium on the twenty-eighth day of December, 1958. The Giants were led by such as Rosey Brown, Andy Robustelli, Rosey Grier, Sam Huff, Harland Svare, Emlen

Tunnell, Chuck Conerly, Frank Gifford, and Kyle Rote. For the Colts, John Unitas, Raymond Berry, Alan Ameche, Lenny Moore, Jim Parker, Big Daddy Lipscomb, and Gino Marchetti.

The Giants represented one of the NFL's oldest, proudest, and most successful franchises. The Colts were a secondhand collection of castoffs and Ewbank reminded them of this. "Many of you are here because other teams didn't want you. Now you can show them," he told the squad.

The Colts had another psychological weapon to counter the Giants' home-field advantage. Earlier in the season they had lost to the Giants, 24-21, when Unitas was out with his injury. George Shaw had thrown three touchdown passes for Baltimore in the defeat and after that season, presumably impressed by this performance, the Giants traded for him. Although Ewbank pleaded with Shaw to remain and enjoy at least the next decade as Johnny U's backup, Shaw insisted on the trade so he could get a chance to play. Ewbank knew the opportunity would expose Shaw's weaknesses. After four seasons with three different teams, the redhead from Oregon drifted out of football.

The Giants' Charley Conerly this season had a ghost-written column syndicated in newspapers under his name. After their victory over the Colts, Conerly's postgame column said the Giants had "out-gutted" Baltimore for the decision. A clipping of that column, reproduced larger than life, was prominently displayed on the Colts' bulletin board all week.

There were 64,185 fans in the historic ball park for the climactic contest. Sixteen thousand of them were up from Baltimore and the visitors let out a collective groan when the Colts blew a big chance to go ahead as Steve Myrha's twenty-seven-yard field goal attempt was blocked by Sam Huff.

They didn't know at the time that this failure would help dictate a lot of the Colts' future strategy.

Late in the first quarter the Giants moved in front, 3-0, on a thirty-six-yard field goal by Pat Summerall, but Ewbank was not distressed. He liked the way his team was moving the ball even though the Colts hadn't scored.

This situation was soon remedied, thanks to a pair of critical fumbles by Frank Gifford, the Giants' handsome and gifted halfback.

The first Gifford fumble was recovered by Baltimore defensive end Ray Krouse at the Giants' twenty. Five running plays later, Ameche scored from the two and Myrha converted for a 7-3 Baltimore lead.

The Colts' defense held on the next series but then Jackie Simpson fumbled Don Chandler's punt and the Giants recovered at the Baltimore ten. However, on the very next play, Gifford fumbled again and Don Joyce recovered for Baltimore at the fourteen. From here, Unitas directed a fourteen-play drive climaxed by a fifteen-yard touchdown pass to Berry for a 14-3 half-time lead.

When play resumed, the Colts appeared to be in a position to lock things up when they drove to a first down at the Giant three midway in the third period. Three runs produced only two yards and on fourth down Ewbank threw away the percentage book that insisted he go for the field goal. Perhaps remembering Myrha's earlier failure and his history of inconsistency, Ewbank called for a sweep by Ameche. But the Giants read the play and Cliff Livingston threw the Horse for a four-yard loss.

Only later would the Colts complain about poor footing where that area of the field had frozen during the afternoon. Not only had the Colts come up with nothing on their long drive, but the Giants garnered a psychological lift from their goal-line stand.

Three plays later, the Giants got a major lucky break. On third-and-two from his thirteen, Conerly passed to Kyle Rote, who took the ball at midfield and ran it down to the Colt twenty-five. Rote fumbled when he was hit, but teammate Alex Webster snatched the loose ball and advanced it twenty-four yards further to the Baltimore one. From this point Mel Triplett rammed it in for the touchdown and Summerall converted to cut Baltimore's lead to 14-10.

With this sequence of events, the momentum shifted totally to the Giants. As thousands of their fans screamed encouragement, the once-scorned Conerly became the master craftsman behind his rugged offensive line. Picking the Colts' defense apart, he connected on consecutive passes to Bob Schnelker for seventeen yards, to Schnelker again for forty-six and, finally, to Gifford for fifteen and a touchdown and a 17-14 lead fifty-three seconds into the final period.

The action was inconclusive most of the fourth quarter, but with less than three minutes to go the Giants found themselves facing the biggest decision of the game. They were third-and-four at their own forty and called on Gifford to sweep right end. If he made the first down, they probably would be able to run the clock on their victory. If he failed, they probably would have to punt and give Johnny Unitas, the most feared passer in football, another shot.

Gifford took the ball and swept past the line of scrimmage, but Marchetti broke through to slow him down and then Lipscomb came across for the final crunching tackle. It was close, so close. An official, head linesman Charley Berry, planted his foot to mark the spot of Gifford's furthest advance. The Giants were stunned. They thought Gifford had fallen forward further than that, perhaps a yard further. Then Berry spotted the ball and there are some Giants who today will privately say that here another goof was committed. Instead of spotting the ball to line up with his toe, as he had intended, they claimed after looking at the movies that Berry put the ball even with his heel. These inches provided the coup de grace. When they brought out the chains to measure, the Giants were inches short.

"I think I made it," Gifford said afterwards. "I fell far enough forward but the official moved it back a yard."

Berry said that Gifford's knee had touched the ground where he had spotted the ball, which is why he moved it back.

Considering that the winners in this game received $4,718 while the losers settled for $3,111, Vince Lombardi, then a Giant assistant coach, grumbled later, "Those six inches were worth $1,600."

While this drama was going on, one Colt was not up watching the measurement. Gino Marchetti was writhing on the ground with a broken right ankle. Lipscomb had fallen on his leg while tackling Gifford and broke the bone in two places. Marchetti's father back in San Francisco had always feared for his son's safety while playing football. He never watched a game. On this December day he made an exception to look in on television. And his boy broke a leg.

Faced with a fourth-and-one from his own forty-three, Giant coach Jim Lee Howell had to make the decision. If he tried for the first down and failed, the Colts would be almost in range to try for the tying field goal. They used Myrha for short kicks and extra points but they also had a fellow named Bert Rechichar on call for the longies, and the tough Tennessee product merely held the NFL's field goal distance record. (At this time, the goalposts were on the goal line, not ten yards back as today.) On the other hand, the Giants had a superb clutch punter in Don Chandler and a tough defense. Howell never really hesitated before sending in Chandler to punt.

And Chandler came through, too, with a long, high boomer on which Carl Taseff signaled for a fair catch at his own fourteen. With only 1:56 left to play, the Colts were eighty-six yards from defeat. On the sidelines, the always excitable Ewbank was reminding Unitas to go into his two-minute offense.

Unitas and Berry had become masters of the sideline pass from long hours of working together after practice and the Giants knew it. And Unitas knew they knew it. So, instead of going that route, Unitas faked to the sidelines and passed again and again to Berry over the middle.

Three straight completions to Berry chewed up seventy-three yards to the Giant thirteen and now there was time for only one more play. Myrha trotted onto the field. Marchetti, being borne to the locker room, ordered the stretcher bearers to pause at the dugout entrance so he could see the kick. With seven seconds left, Myrha booted a twenty-yard field goal that tied the game.

In Baltimore, a motorist listening to the game on his car radio ran into a pole.

To this point, no championship game in NFL history had ever ended in a tie. Only ten years earlier, the league had put in procedures for sudden death overtime.

After a brief pause, the captains, with Unitas subbing for Marchetti, met at midfield for a new toss of the coin. The Giants won and elected to receive, but the Colts' defense refused to allow them to capitalize on this advantage. It was three downs and out for the Giant offense, and at fourth-and-one from his twenty-nine, Chandler punted a fifty-two-yarder.

The Colts set up at their twenty and Ewbank reminded Unitas that he no longer had to fight the clock.

Dupre, nicknamed Long Gone, ran for eleven on the first

play, but then Unitas found himself third-and-eight and passed to Ameche for just the necessary yardage to keep the drive alive at his own forty-one. Again, after being sacked by Dick Modzelewski for an eight-yard loss, Unitas found himself in a third-and-long situation from his thirty-six. This time he called for a pass to Lenny Moore, but the shifty halfback was covered and Unitas just barely got off a throw to Berry before being smashed to the ground again. However, the pass was good for a first down to the Giant forty-three and the Colts were still moving.

Unitas always called his own game with the Colts. He was a master tactician. On the pass to Berry while looking for a secondary receiver and under heavy pressure, he still managed to notice that Giant middle linebacker Sam Huff was lining up a little deeper than usual to help defend against those short passes to Ameche and Moore.

After hitting Berry, Unitas in the huddle called for another pass over the middle to one of his ends. However, as he hunched under the center at the line of scrimmage he noticed that Huff was still lining up deeper than usual. That far back, a tackle would have time to block Huff on a running play. The quarterback's computer brain was flashing signals. He recalled that Modzelewski had sacked him only two plays earlier. Unitas guessed the Giants' defensive tackle would be coming hard again.

Unitas would take advantage of Mo's aggressiveness. The man in front of him would let Modzelewski go, another blocker would slam him from the side and use the defender's own momentum to ride him out of the play. If the trap block on Mo worked and if the tackle could nail Huff, the Colts should break a big gainer.

These calculations took less time than is required to read these words. Unitas checked off and changed plays at the line of scrimmage.

As the quarterback explained later in his book on great NFL games, "Everything worked perfectly. Sam hung back and Mo came like a bull. Art Spinney, the guard, trapped him beautifully and our center, Buzz Nutter, blocked Spinney's man, Rosey Grier. George Preas, the tackle, went through and blocked Huff, and Ameche had clear sailing for twenty-three yards."

"As perfect a call as you will ever see," Ewbank marveled.

Ameche's gain moved the ball to the Giants' twenty and two plays later Unitas hit Berry on a slant pattern for a first down at the eight.

Again Unitas came to the sidelines and this time Ewbank reminded him to "give it to Alan" and play it safe. In sudden death, a field goal wins just as easily as a touchdown.

On first down, Unitas followed orders, a fullback plunge by Ameche that gained a yard. On the sidelines, Ewbank thought, "That's right. Two more like this and we kick the field goal."

Seconds later, though, Ewbank's calm crumbled. Unitas was dropping back to pass. Heresy. Football heresy. Visions of doom and disaster flashed through Ewbank's mind like a speeded-up film clip from *Nightmare Alley*. The worst was the thought of the Colts' pass protection breaking down— Unitas is hit—he fumbles—a Giant picks up the loose ball and runs ninety yards for the winning touchdown. Ewbank was exhausted in the few seconds Unitas required to drop back and loft the ball over two defenders into the arms of Jim Mutscheller. Mutscheller was at the sidelines and stepped out of bounds at the one.

It was a gutty call, an arrogant call. Unitas had seen that the Giants were taking away the inside on Mutscheller. If there was any chance of an interception, he would have thrown the ball away out of bounds.

"Weren't you taking a chance?" he was asked later.

"You're never taking a chance when you know what you're doing," he answered coldly.

Down at the one, it was a piece of Maryland crab cake. Unitas called for Ameche off right tackle, and on the thirteenth play of this eighty-yard drive the Horse stampeded through a huge hole led by Lenny Moore's block. No extra points are kicked in sudden death overtime. The Colts, by a 23-17 score, were champions of the world, only eight minutes and fifteen seconds behind Ewbank's five-year schedule.

The game ball was presented to Marchetti, lying on the trainer's table and waiting for his teammates to close out the victory. As for Ewbank, he was rewarded by Rosenbloom with a $25,000 bonus and a new self-perpetuating three-year contract. Some 30,000 fans greeted the Colts at the airport when they returned, and grateful (and wealthy) fans provided a $50,000 bonus for them to divide. All told, the victory was worth about $10,000 a man to the Colts.

To this point, this was probably the greatest football game ever played and certainly had the greatest impact of any game on the sport's future. It was witnessed by millions on television and firmly established pro football to the nation. Within a decade, players would be getting more than twice $10,000 for winning a championship and they wouldn't require fans to sweeten the pot. Salaries would escalate along with gate receipts and television revenues.

Also, around the nation in their separate homes and clubs, rich young men would watch this game, read of it, and yearn to be a part of this exciting sport themselves. When they found the doors of the NFL closed to them, these men would form their own league to go into operation within two years.

Yet, there also was a cloud on this game. The Colts were favored to win by four points. They could have won with a field goal almost any time before Ameche's plunge, yet Unitas had risked all with his second-down pass to Mutscheller. The wise guys pointed out that Baltimore bettors would have lost their wagers with only a three-point victory. And there were darker rumors. Rosenbloom, admittedly a heavy bettor in other areas, himself had given the points, the sharpies whispered.

Ewbank explained the finish simply by pointing out that neither he nor any of the Colts had much confidence in Myrha. Myrha had been erratic all season. Just before the Giants blocked his first-period field goal attempt, he had misfired from around the thirty-two only to be given another chance because the Giants were off side. And Ewbank also conceded that Unitas was a superb pressure passer, convinced that on any play he could complete any pass, or at least throw it away for minimal damage.

Five years later, when Commissioner Pete Rozelle suspended two players, Paul Hornung and Alex Karras, for betting on their own teams, the Rosenbloom rumors surfaced again. To quell charges of a double standard for players and owners, Rozelle was forced to conduct a full investigation of the old whispers. Soon after, Rozelle reported that the accusations were "unfounded." The commissioner pointed out that although Rosenbloom had admitted heavy gambling on other sports, "no proof whatever has been uncovered" that he had bet on NFL games since becoming an owner.

There are some, however, who believe the Colts' owner feels he should have been cleared more quickly and in stronger terms. They say this incident may have been the genesis of Rosenbloom's subsequent feud with Rozelle, a battle that led to some of the few humiliating defeats on CR's personal scorecard.

Whatever, at this point, there were no real clouds hanging

over Baltimore's harbor. The Colts were champs, and just to show it was no fluke they did it again in '59, the hard way. Down by two games to San Francisco in their division with five weeks to go, they averaged thirty-seven points a game in winning their way home. Two of those final five victories came over the fading Forty-niners. Then, in a title rematch against the Giants before 57,545 fans in Baltimore, they trailed 9-7 going into the final period and won it, 31-16, with a twenty-four-point explosion.

In Ewbank's words, truly this was Baltimore's time to "be known." The Colts were heroes, nationally as well as in their own venue. The team was rich, the players good-looking. Surely all the bad times, all the controversy were in the past.

4

"The Best Part Was
Getting Out"

Bert Jones grew acquainted with defeat in high school and with adversity in college and he never learned to be comfortable with either teammate.

As a high school football player, he joined the varsity his sophomore year and was called upon for duty only when Ruston faced a passing situation. Still, the team did well enough to make the state play-offs.

For the next two years—with his mother charting Bert's performance so she could forward the reports to Dub in Cleveland—Ruston struggled. It was a small school with just enough enrollment to qualify for the top bracket of Louisiana high school competition. Every opponent had more students from which to draw. Bert was barely a .500 quarterback in two seasons as a regular.

Meanwhile, in nearby Shreveport, another quarterback named Joe Ferguson was knocking 'em dead for Woodlawn High. Woodlawn had been utilizing a wide-open passing offense since the days of Terry Bradshaw and so Ferguson was able to compile some eye-catching statistics. Ruston, generally outmanned, favored a more conservative attack, which did little for Bert's reputation among college recruiters.

There are two somewhat conflicting accounts of Bert's decision to attend Louisiana State University.

The prevailing version in Louisiana is that Jones waited until Ferguson, the more highly sought-after, finally accepted a bid to go to Arkansas before making his own commitment to accept a scholarship form LSU. The implication is that Jones wanted to avoid competing with Ferguson for a starting job, or at least wanted to avoid a situation where one of them would be forced to sit on the bench or they would have to share duty.

Jones, as one might expect, disputes this account. He insists that the decision to keep them apart was made mainly by the colleges themselves and that he got the worst of it. In other words, most schools that hoped to enroll Ferguson did not make an active effort to recruit Jones, which makes sense. The two boys lived near each other and were friends. In the recruiting game, the classic ploy is to convince your blue chipper that he alone can save Bullhorn U.'s football program. This can work, though, only if he doesn't know that a dozen other quarterbacks are being enrolled on the same premise. But the fact is, LSU did mount an all-out campaign to get Ferguson and even enlisted the governor of Louisiana in a futile attempt to keep the quarterback from crossing the state line into Arkansas. After Ferguson chose Arkansas, Jones signed with LSU.

"I didn't really have too many options, only about twenty offers," Bert remembers. "That thing about waiting for Joe to make his choice is not true, although it would have been a waste of talent for both of us to go to the same school. I know some schools recruited him and so would not recruit me and I think I got the short end of the stick on that.

"I wanted to go to a school near home and that's why I turned down Notre Dame. I would have gone to Alabama or Arkansas—but they didn't recruit me. So that left LSU."

Jones feels Ferguson had the big advantage back then because he "was almost as good when he got out of high school as he is now, whereas I was just a gangly kid. Actually, everybody in my family matures late. I threw hard, but I wasn't the polished quarterback Joe was."

Still, Bert had plenty of confidence in his ability and he knew that in the right setting, with the right supporting cast, he was just as good as Ferguson. Ferguson, playing for the Louisiana high school champions, made all-state. Bert, playing for a loser, was runner-up.

"He was Mr. Everything, I was Mr. Nothing, but I always felt I had just as much ability—or more," Bert insists.

The decision to enroll at Louisiana State—while not a mistake, as subsequent events proved—was not a happy one for Bert Jones.

Of course, there was the normal homesickness. Bert, still the quiet one, had a difficult time adjusting to noisy, rough-and-tumble dormitory life 200 miles away from home. It was his first time away from the family and he was the first in his family to leave home to attend college.

And, although Baton Rouge is not the largest city in America, it is a city. Bert already had learned to love the outdoor life. At LSU he could not flee at will to woods and field to revive his spirit.

In a football sense, Bert's stay was even less rewarding. Charley McClendon, LSU's head coach, is a big, burly man who prefers his football the same way—tough defense, ram-it-down-their-throats offense. No mistakes, and that means no passing. The pro style of finesse, misdirection, and long, floating passes through the chill night air of Baton Rouge's Tiger Stadium was anathema to Charley Mac. Even the thought gave him a rash.

He had Bert Jones for three years and, according to the quarterback, never played him more than half the time! In a candid moment, Jones once confessed that he almost transferred out of LSU to a school he will not name. He had, in fact, taken every step necessary to transfer short of telling McClendon goodbye.

Asked the high point of his college career, he responded bluntly, "Getting out."

"There were trying times," he reminisced. "I was there three [varsity] years and never played more than half the time. I don't think it [McClendon's offense] was quite as conducive to my style of play. If it was a pressing situation, I was there. I was always the quarterback, but I never played all the time. Can you imagine me here [in Baltimore] and only playing half the time? It was the same sort of situation."

McClendon, for his part, was never completely enamored of Jones. Perhaps he resented this cocky kid with the cannon arm who in many ways was more familiar with sophisticated football and its practitioners than he was. Maybe Bert thought those summers at Hiram, Ohio, had taught him more than in fact they had. But McClendon is on record as saying that Bert was hard to coach in his early years at LSU. He felt Bert thought he knew all there was to know about quarterbacking.

"Bert came to LSU with a strong arm and strong convictions," McClendon would say later. "He had been exposed to the pro game and he was pretty set in his ideas. What I'm saying is, he wasn't the most coachable boy we've ever had."

Actually, Bert was supposed to be red-shirted his sophomore year. This is a practice whereby good prospects are withheld from varsity competition for one season to preserve an extra year of eligibility for a time when they, presumably, are more mature. The NCAA allows athletes five years from enrollment in which to play four seasons.

The year before Jones joined the varsity, McClendon had committed himself to a dual quarterback philosophy. As Bert approached his sophomore season he ranked behind senior Buddy Lee, later to play briefly with the pros, and junior Butch Duhe. If all went well, Lee and Duhe would do the quarterbacking and Jones could safely be red-shirted.

However, just ten days before the season, Duhe, only twenty years old, died suddenly of an aneurism in the brain. The tragic event made it necessary for Bert to play as a sophomore.

Bert showed his toughness that season. He played 40 percent of the time even though hobbled by a bad knee. He had hurt the knee just before the opener but played the season through even though he says the joint had to be drained of excess fluid—a painful procedure—every other day. After the season it required two operations before he could play again.

The Tigers did make it to the Orange Bowl that season, but Bert didn't improve his relations with McClendon any when he shook off a play from the bench and then threw an interception on his own call to kill an LSU drive in the 17-12 loss to Nebraska.

Jones welcomed the postseason surgery. "I knew how much it hurt to play all season with an injured knee and I knew the operation was my way out. It was my salvation," he said. "I never thought I would never play again."

There was more frustration in store during Bert's junior

season. Paul Lyons, a high school quarterback who had been playing defense for LSU, was moved back to offense and eventually ahead of Jones at quarterback. Lyons was a roll-out quarterback. He had none of Bert's physical skills, especially as a passer, but the team seemed to respond to his leadership and McClendon never liked to throw the ball anyway if he could help it. Lyons was 5-10, 190. Bert was 6-3, 205 and ran the forty yards in a swift 4.7 seconds. His arm was so strong he once almost threw the football out of Tiger Stadium. ("I missed by five rows of seats; our punter missed by twenty," Bert once confessed.) But McClendon was convinced that the nifty Lyons could run his offense better and he installed him as starting quarterback after Jones threw three interceptions in a 31-21 opening loss to Colorado.

From then until the tenth game of the season, Bert played only when the Bengals got behind and needed his throwing arm.

Game ten was on national television in prime time against Notre Dame. LSU could make a name for itself in this one.

Five minutes before the kickoff, McClendon, as he later would admit, "played a hunch." He tabbed Jones as his starting quarterback. Bert responded by completing seven of nine passes for two touchdowns in a 28-8 victory.

From then on he was LSU's number one quarterback even though McClendon still insisted that he share the time. In the Sun Bowl that season he was 12 for 18 passing in a 33-15 victory over Iowa State.

Bert's greatest college game took place during his senior season against arch-rival Mississippi.

By this time, McClendon was saying things like, "Now Bert is more aware of the facts of life, aware of the overall picture. He has always been highly intelligent. Maturity is what did it."

Quarterback coach Charlie Pevey, who played at LSU with the legendary Y. A. Tittle, agreed: "Age helped Bert mature physically. Increased confidence matured him mentally. Bert is the finest passer I've been around. Tittle was a great one. He had a great touch. But Bert is bigger and stronger and he's got the best arm I've seen, period."

Tiger Stadium is one of the wildest football arenas in the nation. The home games are played at night, which seems to increase the frenzy, as partisan cheers and screams echo off the wall of darkness without. The stadium is always sold out and when they roll out Mike, the school's Bengal Tiger mascot, in his cage, the crowd responds with almost primeval enthusiasm. Imagine if they had lights in the Roman Coliseum, Lions versus Christians in the main event. The folks in Baton Rouge would still make more noise, especially against a neighbor Southeastern Conference rival like Ole Miss.

This was the pressure situation Bert faced before 67,500 screaming fans—as in fanatics—going into the last two minutes against Mississippi with LSU trailing, 16-10.

With eighty seconds to play, the Bayou Bengals moved to offense at their own twenty. They had no time-outs remaining. "Don't worry, we're going to get it," Bert told his teammates in the huddle—and not one doubted him.

Down the field Jones drove his team until, with the clock stopped and showing only one second, he had moved the ball to the Rebel ten. The next play, number thirteen on the drive, would be the last of the game.

Outwardly calm, Bert went to the sideline to confer with McClendon. From all reports, honest, this is what the coach said:

"Son, this is it."

"As if I didn't know," Bert thought to himself as he wiped his fingers on a towel. He headed toward the huddle, then turned suddenly back to McClendon—and winked.

"We're going to score now," Bert told his teammates as he called another pass play in the huddle. And then he dropped back and lofted a soft ten-yarder over the linebackers to sophomore running back Brad Davis. The horn signaling the end of the game went off as the play was unfolding. Bert never heard it. In a sense, the Tigers had scored after the game was over.

The touchdown, however, only made it 16-16. LSU would still be allowed to try the extra point. With the clock showing zeros and the stadium for once hushed, Rusty Jackson kicked the extra point in a heart-stopping 17-16 victory.

By the time he finished his senior season, Jones had set twenty school records, made virtually every All-America team, led all quarterbacks in voting for the Heisman Trophy (Johnny Rodgers won it), and his No. 7 jersey was going to be retired. He had converted McClendon, too, and the pro scouts already were sold. There was little doubt he would be the first quarterback chosen in the upcoming professional draft and maybe the first player to be picked.

One man who wasn't surprised at Bert's development was Eddie Robinson, respected head coach at Grambling and a man who had sent dozens of players to the pros. Robinson and Dub Jones had been close friends for years. Dub had been a great help to Grambling's football program back when such voluntary interracial gestures weren't exactly fashionable in northern Louisiana. But Dub never looked at it that way, of course, and Eddie Robinson even tried to recruit Bert to play for his predominantly black team. After all, it was only a three-mile commute.

"Bert would have made me a helluva coach," Robinson says often with a fond smile. "After all, how could he miss? The boy was practically born on a football field. He was watching films of his daddy running pass routes when other kids were watching cartoons."

5

The Loss Was Guaranteed

—

Soon after his Colts beat the Giants for their second straight championship, Weeb Ewbank did some research. No NFL team had ever won more than two titles in a row. He wondered why. He studied all of these two-time winners, the Bears of 1940–41, the Eagles of 1948–49, the Lions of 1952–53, the Browns of 1954–55.

Was there a common denominator in their failure to make it three straight?

Ewbank thought so. Winning a championship requires an experienced team of a certain age. These are the kind of players a coach must start thinking about replacing. Yet how do you replace a man who obviously has been playing at championship form? Teams that win together grow old together.

Weeb didn't want that to happen to him, but what are you gonna do? Fire Unitas and Ameche and Marchetti?

Whatever his misgivings, Ewbank went into 1960 with pretty much a pat hand. Although Unitas was playing with a fractured vertebra, the Colts held a one-game lead over Green Bay going into the ninth game of the season. But then Alan Ameche went down with a torn Achilles tendon. In only his sixth season as a pro, Ameche's career was over. So were the Colts' title hopes as they lost their last four.

The third-year jinx had struck again.

Meanwhile, two new forces were emerging in the sixties that would make life more difficult for the Colts and Weeb Ewbank.

One was that new kid on the block, the American Football League, the first challenge to the NFL since the All-America Conference had created these Colts and then faded away ten years before. This new league would have two major advantages over its short-lived predecessor—a television contract that provided the crucial financial cushion and a national appetite for pro football that the NFL, locked smugly for the last ten years in a twelve-team format, could not satisfy.

The other change was the arrival in 1959 of Vince Lombardi in Green Bay. Lombardi, for years a top assistant with the Giants, was given complete control of the Packers and the franchise bloomed. His 1960 team captured the league's Western Division championship but lost in the play-offs. They would win the next two league titles, though, and over the next seven seasons dominated pro football with five championships.

Ewbank's Colts lost many college prospects in the talent war with the new AFL and, within their league, faced fierce competition even to win in their own division from the Packers.

As the 1961 season approached, the Colts traded Big Daddy Lipscomb, the crude but likable giant, and troublesome cornerback Johnny Sample to the Steelers. Art Donovan, the other tackle, found himself playing that one season too long. The Colts' defense was aging and few replacements were in sight. The college draft, diluted with the addition of two new NFL teams by expansion and competition from the AFL, was not productive.

Weeb and the Colts finished 1961 with an 8-6 record but the next year dropped to 7-7. Rosenbloom summarily fired Ewbank.

Ironically, that same season Cleveland also discharged its founding and namesake coach, Paul Brown. Brown had brought Ewbank into professional coaching in Cleveland but their relationship went further back than that. They once were teammates at Miami of Ohio, the collegiate cradle of coaches. Both were quarterbacks. Brown, as a transfer student, was a year behind Ewbank in eligibility and sat on the bench while Weeb started. For the rest of their lives their relationship was that of friends and rivals, with first one aspect dominant and then the other, like interchangeable theatrical masks.

Why did Rosenbloom fire his legendary coach, the man who had done so much for his franchise—and his investment?

The evidence is that he felt Ewbank had lost control of his veteran players. His schoolmasterish approach worked with rookies and his stolid patience and organizational skill were unsurpassed when it came to building a franchise.

But, as the team stabilized and players grew more worldly, these veterans demanded straight answers rather than vague homilies from their coach. Years later Weeb would repeat the same pattern with the Jets.

Still, there were many in football who thought Ewbank deserved a chance to fight his way out of the Colts' mild slump. After all, 7-7 wasn't exactly a disgrace.

The critical factor in the firing was Rosenbloom, his impatience and his vanity. He had almost fired Weeb before and Ewbank never did fit your image of the tough, dynamic head coach. In private conversation with veteran players like Unitas, Rosenbloom referred to Ewbank as "the weasel." Weeb's circumlocution exasperated Rosenbloom as well as his players. Rosenbloom, who took the Colts' failure to keep winning as a personal reflection, was in a position to do something about it.

Considering all Ewbank had done for the franchise, the method Rosenbloom used in discharging him did not reflect very highly on the Colts' owner. As the disappointing season drew to an end, Ewbank met with his boss. Weeb had that self-perpetuating contract but in fairness to his assistants who might be fired with no such security, he wanted to know what Rosenbloom had in mind.

"You've got no worries," Rosenbloom is supposed to have told Ewbank, who then left with a free mind to scout the Senior Bowl workouts and game in Mobile, Alabama. Because his wife, Lucy, is afraid to fly, they took the train.

According to Paul Zimmerman's fine book about Weeb, the Ewbanks were on the train returning to Baltimore when Rosenbloom called the press conference to announce the firing.

Ewbank says he arrived in Baltimore at 4:00 A.M. and was called by a newsman at 7:00 to get his reaction to being fired. Weeb, of course, was flabbergasted. He didn't know what was happening. The reporter told him a press conference had been called for 11:00 that morning. Rosenbloom then summoned Ewbank to his office at about 9:00 o'clock and in a terse conversation that supposedly lasted little more than two minutes, Weeb was out. So much for gratitude. By this action Rosenbloom proved the Colts were truly one man's family. Weeb was not out of work for long, however. Three months and one week after being relieved in Baltimore he was named head coach and general manager of the New York Jets by the syndicate that had just taken over the bankrupt Titans of the AFL. "I've seen sicker cows than this get well," Ewbank said on assuming the job, in a reference to his first seasons with the secondhand Colts. Rosenbloom, who had recommended Weeb to the Jets, would come to rue that analogy.

To replace Ewbank, Rosenbloom once again reached into the ranks of NFL assistants and made Detroit's defensive coordinator, Don Shula, at age thirty-three the youngest head coach in league history.

Shula, who attended John Carroll University in Cleveland, grew up with the Browns and played for them before being traded to the Colts in 1953. He spent four seasons under Ewbank as a defensive back before finishing up his career in Washington in 1957.

It was a tribute to Shula's tenaciousness and intelligence that he played as long as he did. He wasn't that fast and he wasn't that big, but he was tough and he was smart and he worked hard. He brought all these attributes plus an explosive Hungarian temper to his coaching.

Shula's first season of 1963, the Colts were only 8-6. But they won their last three games and five of their last six as such fine young players as Tom Matte, Jerry Hill, Bob Vogel, John Mackey, Fred Miller, and Johnny Logan began to mature.

By his second year, Shula had the Colts flying. After losing their opener to Minnesota, the Colts reeled off eleven straight victories to win the Western Conference championship with a 12-2 record. In the title game they bowed to the Browns, 27-0.

Shula produced one of his best coaching jobs in 1964. The Colts won their opener, lost to Green Bay, and then marched to eight victories in a row before tying Detroit.

A week later, however, in a 13-0 loss to the Bears, John Unitas was lost for the season with a damaged knee. And the following week, replacement Gary Cuozzo followed him to the sidelines with a dislocated shoulder.

It was too late for the Colts to come up with a suitable outside replacement, although they did sign veteran Ed Brown for emergency duty.

With one game left, Brown had no time to learn the offense or the personnel and so Tom Matte, the intense, ulcer-plagued halfback, was tapped to start at quarterback. Matte had played the position before as a collegian for run-oriented Ohio State five years earlier, but even then he was not known as a passer. The Buckeyes' irascible Woody Hayes looked on the forward pass with even more distaste than LSU's Charley McClendon.

The Colts' entire offense, of course, was geared around Johnny Unitas and his golden arm, but at this point Shula had little choice. Matte was given a few days of practice and, with a list of suggested plays inked onto his wristbands, he led the Colts to a shocking 20-17 victory over the Rams in Los Angeles.

That victory earned the Colts a tie for first place in the NFL's Western Division with Green Bay as both teams finished with 10-3-1 records. A play-off was scheduled in the frigid Wisconsin city for the day after Christmas.

Again Matte with his annotated wristbands was at quarterback for the Colts, who took a 7-0 lead in the first quarter when Don Shinnick recovered a Bill Anderson fumble and ran it in from twenty-five yards out for a touchdown. Bart Starr, the Packers' quarterback, was injured on that play and so Green Bay also had to go the route with a substitute. Only in this case it was not a converted halfback, but the poised and canny veteran, Zeke Bratkowski.

Still, by half time, the Colts had expanded their lead to 10-0 on a fifteen-yard field goal by Lou Michaels.

But with Matte completing only two of twelve passes for the day, the Colts could score no more. The Packers got on the board with a one-yard touchdown run by Paul Hornung in the third period and then tied the score on a twenty-two-yard field goal by Don Chandler, the old Giant, with only 1:58 remaining in the fourth quarter.

Once again the Colts were involved in a sudden death title game. For almost a full period their inspired defense kept the Packers at bay as 50,485 fans shivered in frigid Lambeau Field and wondered when it all would end.

The first overtime period was drawing to a close when the Packers once again moved deep into Baltimore territory. Once again they called on Chandler, purchased just that season from the Giants, who had used him exclusively as a punter.

This time Chandler lined up at the twenty-five, dug his toe into the heavy, near-frozen football, and then watched anxiously as his high kick began to slice dangerously toward the right upright. Often in this situation a kicker will know almost immediately if he has been successful and either confidently walk away or throw his hands into the air, depending on the emotion of the moment. Chandler did not move. He was unsure; the ball had passed high over the upright. Finally, after what seemed like long minutes, the referee raised his hands up in the air to signify a successful field goal and a 13-10 Packer victory after 13:39 of overtime.

Perhaps because of the cold, the Colts took their defeat numbly at first. But as they thawed out on the trip home, their rage grew. They became more and more convinced that Chandler's kick had been wide and should not have counted. To this day they still insist that is so. They claimed that some of the Packers privately agreed with them. They ranted, they raved. The score remained unchanged.

By the next year, though, NFL rules did change. The uprights, previously twenty feet high, would be extended another ten feet.

Matte's famous wristbands went to the Pro Football Hall of Fame in Canton, Ohio. The Packers went on to beat Cleveland for the first of three straight NFL championships.

In June of 1966, the war between the two football leagues was ended with a merger. Only this time it was not a case of the NFL grudgingly agreeing to absorb the most attractive survivors of its beaten rival. The AFL that spring had changed its tactics. Instead of competing merely for the best college prospects, the young league waged an aggressive campaign to lock up established NFL stars for future delivery when their current contracts expired. Commissioner Al Davis vowed he would steal away every established quarterback no matter how high the ransom. Quickly NFL owners made secret overtures to arrange a truce and an eventual merger.

Player raids were dropped even though some NFL veterans had to be paid off, a common college draft was agreed upon for the following year, and to climax this first season of peace, there would be an event football fans had long been awaiting, a Super Bowl between the two champions.

The Packers, who finished three games ahead of Baltimore in the standings, won the honor of representing the NFL in Super Bowl I and routed Kansas City in the first meeting, 35-10. The next year the Colts came closer. Only one other team in the NFL matched their 11-1-2 record, but that team happened to be the Rams of their own division. A 34-10 Los Angeles victory over Baltimore in the final game of the season gave the Rams the advantage in breaking the tie.

The Colts, despite their fine record, didn't even go to the play-offs.

There would be no such denials or frustration in 1968.

By this time the Colts had completed a thorough rebuilding of their first championship team although Unitas remained as the kingpin quarterback, still the master of the unexpected, daring maneuver that left defenders frozen in awe. Raymond Berry had retired with the all-time pass-receiving championship and others like Lenny Moore and Jim Parker had joined such as Marchetti and Donovan in retirement. Unitas still had John Mackey, regarded by many as the greatest tight end in history, and the defense, always Shula's favorite platoon, was ramrodded by such young stars as monstrous Bubba Smith in the line and reckless Mike Curtis at linebacker.

Yes, Unitas was still the kingpin, but where was Unitas? The Golden Arm had been nursing a tarnished elbow in training camp. In desperation, only weeks before the opener, Shula sent a fourth-round draft choice and an obscure tight end named Butch Wilson to the Giants for a much-traveled veteran quarterback, Earl Morrall.

Morrall, who already had played for four different NFL teams in a twelve-year career, was deemed washed up at the age of thirty-four. (He finally retired under duress after the 1976 season. One reason for his longevity may have been his insistence despite advancing years and changing fashions on clinging to the crewcut hair style of his youth.)

Shula hoped that Morrall could fill in for a couple of games until Unitas's sore arm recovered, but John was slow in healing and the Colts kept winning with Earl.

Only twice all season was Unitas a factor. He tested his arm in game six and threw three interceptions while completing only one of eleven passes in a 30-20 loss to Cleveland.

That would be the Colts' only defeat of the regular season. And in the last game of the year he signaled he was ready when he came off the bench to break a 14-14 tie with his only two touchdown passes of the season for a 28-24 victory over the Rams.

Otherwise, it was all Morrall and defense as the Colts compiled a 13-1 record that included an eight-game winning streak down the stretch. To make the season doubly sweet for Morrall, the thirteen victories included decisions over all four of the teams that had previously cast him aside—San Francisco, Pittsburgh, the Giants, and Detroit.

Just as important as Morrall, and perhaps more so, was the unbending defense that produced three shutouts and in one four-game stretch did not allow a touchdown. In fourteen games, the Colts outscored their opponents 402 points to 144.

The Colts were just as awesome in the first two rounds of the play-offs. They had Minnesota 21-0 in the fourth quarter before packaging a 24-10 victory in the cold and rain at home in the first round. The next week, before more than 80,000 fans in Cleveland, they humiliated the Browns, 34-0, for the NFL championship and the right to play in Super Bowl III. Tom Matte scored three touchdowns, two in a seventeen-point second period, for Baltimore. This was only the second shutout in the Browns' proud history.

Truly, Carroll Rosenbloom could not be blamed for thinking this was the greatest Colt team of all time, maybe the greatest football team of all time.

Meanwhile, in the so-called other league, strange things were happening. The New York Jets, with their brash $400,-000 quarterback, Joe Namath, had breezed to their division championship with an 11-3 record. Then, in a dramatic play-off, the Jets beat Oakland, 27-23, for the American Football

League title. NFL officials had been so certain of a Jet defeat in that game they hadn't even bothered to discuss contingency plans for the Super Bowl with that team's representatives.

The odds-makers took out their adding machines for this one. They looked at the AFL's record in the past two Super Bowls. They scanned the Jets roster and decided this was the weakest AFL representative to make it to this climactic game. They checked out Baltimore's awesome record against supposedly tougher competition and the imposing lineup of stars who had enabled them to dominate their league and the Cleveland Browns with a second-string quarterback.

The Colts were installed as seventeen-point favorites and at times you could get as many as nineteen. It was 7-to-1 odds in a straight bet.

Two important Jets, however, were not impressed.

One of them was the coach, Weeb Ewbank, discarded by this same Baltimore franchise six years before. In many ways, this was still his team; all but a handful had played for him and some of the others were products of his final draft. He searched his memory bank and studied film. To keep his players from being overawed, as had happened to the Chiefs and Raiders in previous Super Bowls against the legendary Packers, he compared each of the Colt starters to a player the Jets had faced in their own league. He also noticed how many of his old Colts had almost imperceptibly started to go downhill. After several days of this, tight end Pete Lammons laughingly asked Ewbank to stop showing them game films of the Colts. "We're getting overconfident," he complained.

The other cocky Jet was Joe Namath himself.

To escape bad weather in New York, Ewbank had brought his team down to balmy Fort Lauderdale to start training

for the game in Miami's Orange Bowl a full ten days early.
He also told his players to bring along their wives and children. "What the hell is Weeb doing?" Don Shula asked as he
questioned the two coaching heresies of early arrival at a
game site and the presence of the families.

As Namath stepped from the Jets' chartered plane on its
arrival in Fort Lauderdale, he told waiting interviewers that
there were at least four or five quarterbacks in the ten-team
AFL more gifted than Earl Morrall—and that included his
own backup, Babe Parilli.

A couple of nights later, Namath charmed his way out of
a potential barroom fistfight with the Colts' belligerent defensive tackle and place-kicker, Lou Michaels, whose brother
Walt was an assistant coach with the Jets. And several days
before the game, Namath stood up at a Miami sports dinner
and told the audience, "I guarantee" the Jets will win on
Sunday.

The Colts, meanwhile, found themselves confident but
confused. The circus atmosphere of Super Bowl week upset
them. Don Shula almost lost his Hungarian temper when
asked about Namath's demeaning remarks about his quarterback. Unitas privately thought the Colts should spend more
time getting him ready to play. He felt he had been ready
to go for a couple of weeks. While Shula yelled and screamed
in practice, Weeb Ewbank, the sly old fox of football, let his
troops prepare with a loose rein.

Shortly before the kickoff, Rosenbloom and Ewbank happened to meet in the Orange Bowl.

Rosenbloom had made preparations for an elaborate victory party at his home nearby in exclusive Golden Beach,
Florida. "I want you and Lucy to be sure to come by after
the game," Rosenbloom said grandly.

"Thanks, Carroll, but I won't be able to make it," Weeb replied.

He was counting on attending his own party.

The first half of Super Bowl III was a mountain of frustration for the Colts.

Lou Michaels missed a twenty-seven-yard field goal attempt at the end of Baltimore's first drive, and after the Colts recovered a Jet fumble at the New York twelve, another scoring opportunity was erased when Randy Beverly intercepted Morrall's tipped pass in the end zone.

Given this reprieve, the Jets drove eighty yards for a touchdown. Fullback Matt Snell, who shredded the Colt defense all day for a record 121 yards rushing, scored from the four. Jim Turner, the argumentative place-kicker, converted for a 7-0 second-quarter lead.

The Colts continued to squander opportunities in the first half. Michaels missed another field goal from the forty-six, and Morrall was intercepted again at the two by Johnny Sample. Yes, the same Johnny Sample discarded years before after playing on a championship team for the Colts.

The Jets were unable to move out after Sample's theft and the Colts' defense forced them to punt from their end zone. With forty-three seconds left in the first half, Balitmore set up at the Jet forty-three.

Jerry Hill gained a yard and then, with twenty-five seconds left, Morrall handed off to Tom Matte on an apparent sweep around right end. Suddenly, however, Matte stopped dead and tossed a long looping lateral back to the quarterback.

It was the old flea-flicker play, a trick maneuver that had been old when Weeb Ewbank first started coaching high school ball in Ohio in the 1930s. In the second game of the season, against Atlanta, the Colts had turned that play into a forty-six-yard touchdown pass from Morrall to Jimmy Orr.

On this day in the Orange Bowl, as more than 75,000 fans gaped in disbelief, Orr again was open down field near the left hash mark. The picture is frozen in memory. Morrall standing there, his arm cocked. Orr, wide open down the field, standing there, frantically waving his arms. Even though, as Shula coldly explained later, "The play is designed for Orr," Morrall didn't see him!

Instead, after what appeared to be interminable seconds, the frozen quarterback spotted his fullback, Jerry Hill, open over the middle. He lofted the ball in that direction, but by the time it arrived, safety Jim Hudson had recovered. He swooped in and intercepted at the twelve. The Colts' hopes of getting on the board in the first half died with that third Jet interception.

At half time, Shula made a decision. He would give Morrall one more chance to move the team, then switch to Unitas. Unitas was quietly alerted.

Shula's plan ran into trouble almost immediately. On the Colts' first offensive play of the third quarter, Matte fumbled to set up a thirty-two-yard Jim Turner field goal for a 10-0 New York lead.

Because of the fumble, Shula felt obliged to give Morrall one more shot. After all, Morrall had brought the Colts this far. He deserved every chance to win the big one.

Once again Morrall came out on the field to lead the offense, but this time there was a different reaction from the crowd. A hum of excited anticipation. The Jets anxiously looked across the field. They could almost sense what was happening. John Unitas, the maestro, in his distinctive No. 19 jersey and old-fashioned high-topped shoes, was warming up behind the Baltimore bench.

Soon he would be coming into the game. Morrall again

failed to move the offense and the Jets came right back with another field goal, a thirty-yarder by Turner for a 13-0 lead before Unitas could get off the bench.

The delay was terribly costly to the Colts. While Shula deferred changing quarterbacks, the Jets had been able to add a pair of field goals. Baltimore now would need two touchdowns to win. Precious minutes on the clock had been wasted. Unitas did not have as much time to rally the Colts.

Still, as the fans cheered his appearance, a spasm of concern swept the Jets across the way. This was a legend walking out onto the field. Unitas was annoyed that he had not been called upon earlier. To this day he still resents Shula's delay. But in the huddle he remained the cool, hard-eyed professional.

The Unitas magic did not work at first. It was three-plays-and-out for the Colt offense as the third period ended. In the entire quarter the Colts had the ball for only seven plays.

As the fourth quarter began, Turner kicked another field goal, from the nine, and now the Jets had a 16-0 cushion. The Colts would need three scores to beat them, but still the upstart New Yorkers could not rest easy. Unitas had overcome larger deficits in less time before. And against teams with more impressive credentials.

Following the Jets' kickoff, the old Unitas reappeared. Deftly and patiently he moved the Colts downfield as if the scoreboard still showed zeros for each team and there was a full game still to play. But on second down from the Jet twenty-five, Johnny U's pass for Orr was intercepted in the end zone by Randy Beverly, the slender free-agent cornerback. It was Beverly's second interception and the fourth of the afternoon for New York.

More precious minutes wasted! Time favored the underdogs now and the Jets made Baltimore pay dearly in that commodity for every yard they bought. Unitas, calling on reserves of toughness that had brought him back from the rocky sandlots of Pittsburgh, drove the Colts to their first touchdown, a one-yard smash by Jerry Hill. But by this time, only 3:19 still showed on the Orange Bowl clock over the open end of the stadium where Michaels had missed his first field goal.

The Colts desperately tried an onside kick and it worked, but they ran out of downs and then they ran out of time as 16-7 losers.

Not just losers, either, but one-sided losers in the biggest upset in professional football history. Carroll Rosenbloom, whose all-consuming passion in life was to be first in everything, had become the first NFL owner to lose a Super Bowl to the Mickey Mouse League.

NFL partisans were stunned. Rosenbloom was in shock. He felt that Ewbank, the man he once discarded as passé, had outcoached his guy. In Rosenbloom's reasoning, Shula had let him down and it may be that he never forgave Don for this.

"We felt we had as fine a football team as had ever been put together and then you wake up and find out that you've been a bunch of bums. It's like finding your wife running around with another guy," Rosenbloom would say much later.

When Weeb Ewbank drove back to Fort Lauderdale for his own victory party, he passed Rosenbloom's house on the beach. It was early, but Carroll's party was already over.

Embarrassing as this defeat may have been, it did provide a financial windfall for Rosenbloom and the Colts.

Before the Jets' victory, the established NFL teams had planned to implement the merger—delayed this long until various TV contracts expired—by retaining the same alignment of teams. There would be sixteen in the NFL, ten in the AFL. Because of the big edge in drafting (six extra players in each round) and the larger pool from which to make preferential waiver claims, the status quo would have assured continuing NFL dominance.

However, flush with newfound self-esteem after the Jets' victory, AFL owners flexed muscles at the next league meeting that spring. They insisted on a true merger, with three NFL teams moving over to their circuit for an even 13-13 split. Eventually, this was done, with the Colts leading the exodus (followed by Pittsburgh and Cleveland) with a $3 million sweetener from their colleagues, effective in 1970.

Weeb Ewbank had helped change the face of football because of the excitement generated by his Colts' overtime victory over the Giants in 1958. A decade later, he played an even more significant role by beating his old club with the underdog Jets.

The Super Bowl loss also changed the face of the Colts. Veteran defensive players like Ordell Braase, Don Shinnick, and Bobby Boyd had suddenly grown old under pressure from the Jets and they retired. Others like Lou Michaels, Dennis Gaubatz, and Lenny Lyles were phased out the following season. Mike Curtis was moved from outside linebacker to a post in the middle to make room for a gangly newcomer named Ted Hendricks.

The Colts in '69 slumped to an 8-5-1 record and second place in their division. Rosenbloom—not so privately—more and more expressed criticism of Shula as a guy who couldn't win the big ones.

Shula is not dumb. He could read the signs. Another poor season and he might be Ewbank-ed. Down in Miami, the expansion Dolphins had completed their fourth season and were looking to make a coaching change. Through an intermediary, they inquired if Shula would be interested in the dual role of coach and general manager. Shula replied affirmatively and the deal was made and signed. All this time Carroll Rosenbloom was vacationing abroad. When he returned and learned what had transpired, he exploded with righteous anger.

He charged the Dolphins had tampered with his head coach, who was still under contract. Miami owner Joe Robbie insisted that with Carroll away he had followed protocol by seeking permission from Rosenbloom's son, Steve, then officially "assistant to the president." He pointed out that it was okay to talk to Shula since Don was moving up to a new level as general manager as well as coach.

The dispute eventually went to Commissioner Pete Rozelle, who ruled that Miami was guilty only of a slight case of tampering because of the initial informal approach through Miami sports writer, Bill Braucher. Braucher had gone to college with Shula. Eventually Rozelle ordered the Dolphins to turn over their next-first round draft choice to Baltimore as compensation.

The swap, of course, turned out to be a bargain for the Dolphins. Baltimore used the draft choice to pick running back Don McCauley, but Miami got one of the great coaches in football. Rosenbloom complained that he had been shortchanged. This may have been the real beginning of his feud with the commissioner.

As a replacement, CR reached down into the Colt staff and promoted an eleven-year assistant, Don McCafferty, to the head job.

Shula was a driver, a screamer. McCafferty took a more relaxed approach. His players called him Easy Rider and they responded to his calm leadership. It was a pleasant change for them.

This was the Colts' first season as members of the newly aligned American Conference of the NFL. With Morrall and Unitas relieving each other and the defense again carrying the load, the Colts won their division championship, but the standings provided a warning for the future. In second place by a mere 1½ games were the once-hapless Miami Dolphins, qualifying for the play-offs for the first time in their history as a wild card team under new coach Don Shula.

The Colts shut out Cincinnati, 17-0, in the first round of the play-offs and qualified for Super Bowl V in Miami by besting Oakland, 27-17, for the AFC championship.

Their opponent would be the Dallas Cowboys, whose success in the NFL's second try in that city had almost made people forget their initial failure, almost two decades earlier, that had created the current Baltimore Colts.

NFL traditionalists pointed out before the game that this Super Bowl matched two of the league's old boys, but once they kicked off the traditionalists had little cause to brag. There were eight fumbles in the game, three pass interceptions, fourteen penalties, a missed field goal, and a blocked extra point. Some called it the Blunder Bowl.

At half time, the Cowboys led, 13-6, but the Colts tied when Rick Volk's interception and thirty-yard return set up a short scoring plunge by Tom Nowatzke in the fourth period. With barely a minute to go it looked as if the Colts might find themselves involved in the third overtime play-off game of their history. But then Mike Curtis intercepted a Craig Morton pass and returned it thirteen yards to the Cowboy twenty-eight. Two plays later, the Colts called on their rookie place-kicker, Jim O'Brien, to try to win it. O'Brien had dreamed during the previous week that a long field goal on the last play of the game would decide Super Bowl V. In his dream, the identity of the kicker was always obscured.

Was it O'Brien or Mike Clark of the Cowboys? He couldn't wait to find out.

In reality, it was to be a wide-awake O'Brien. With five seconds left, he kicked a thirty-two-yarder for a 16-13 Baltimore victory.

There was an irony in this game as Rosenbloom finally collected his Tiffany-designed Super Bowl trophy two years behind schedule. In the second quarter, Johnny Unitas had been driven from action with bruised ribs. The winning Super Bowl pitcher in relief was the goat of the game two years before—crew-cut Earl Morrall.

6
Swap of the Century

—

Success did not bring happiness to Carroll Rosenbloom in Baltimore.

He was unhappy with the condition of city-owned Memorial Stadium, already decaying though only ten years old, and even more displeased with terms of his lease under which he shared occupancy with the baseball Orioles. But mostly he was bitter because Baltimore fans, who had once turned out by the thousands to attend an intrasquad game, were now so sophisticated they declined en masse to pay top prices for preseason exhibition games at home. When he tried to tie in these games with the regular-season ticket package, he was subjected to a vicious battering from the local press.

Although such tie-ins had been ruled legal in several court tests around the nation, Rosenbloom was forced to back down. Three games in 1971 averaged a mere 16,000 fans. Meanwhile, Rosenbloom increased his demands on the city of Baltimore for a new stadium, or at least major improvements in the old. He tried to get promises for a new stadium of his own in the suburbs, outside the city limits, and when these maneuvers failed he openly threatened to move the franchise to Tampa.

Commissioner Pete Rozelle, however, quickly shot down those Colts-to-Tampa threats before they got off the ground. The rift between him and Rosenbloom widened.

Over the years, Rosenbloom had made countless enemies in Baltimore, including influential members of the press. Some, including at least one former employee, had personal reasons for the vendetta, but CR, never strong in PR, made it easy for people to attack him.

One short year after the Super Bowl victory, Rosenbloom and his Colts were under siege in their own hometown.

Under McCafferty's loose grip, the Colts slipped to a 10-4 record in 1971 as Johnny Unitas came back for the second half of the season after undergoing surgery for a torn Achilles tendon. He had hurt himself playing paddle ball in the off-season to get in shape. Still, 10-4 was good enough to make the play-offs as a wild card when Baltimore finished second to Miami in the American Conference Eastern Division. The Colts beat Cleveland, 20-3, in the first round of the play-offs but then lost to the Dolphins, 21-0, for the AFC title, a result that brought immense pleasure to Don Shula but did nothing to improve Rosenbloom's disposition.

About that time, events were transpiring in other NFL circles that would have a tremendous impact on Baltimore and the Colts.

Down in Miami, Joe Thomas, the man who once scouted the talent that had made Minnesota a Super Bowl team, chafed under his dead-end job as director of personnel of the Dolphins. Don Shula was head coach and general manager. Joe Robbie was an active owner who controlled the business side. There was no way for Thomas to advance in Miami. Despite offers of more money and a vice-president's title he resigned even though he didn't have another job.

This was the impulsive style of Joe Thomas, a hard-driving genius at spotting football talent.

Thomas grew up in the rural area outside Warren, Ohio, which is near Youngstown in the northeast corner of the state. He was born in 1921 and that meant he was old enough to understand the frightening insecurities of the Great Depression of the thirties. This fear never left him. No position was ever secure enough; demons followed like shadows waiting to foreclose on whatever corner in life he had staked out.

Thomas played football at Ohio Northern and served in the Navy in World War II. The struggles of his early coaching career could be summed up by a list of his simultaneous duties at DePauw University for four years: assistant coach in football, assistant coach in basketball, head coach in baseball. He probably still had trouble making ends meet even though he was unmarried.

Weeb Ewbank brought Thomas into pro football as defensive line coach and an assistant in the personnel department with the Colts in 1954. After several stops along the way, he became the first person hired by the expansion Minnesota Vikings in 1960 to find them the ingredients for a winning team.

Five years later he moved to Miami, but now he was out of work. He had hoped to land the general manager's job in St. Louis but at the last minute they named another man. The future looked bleak, but Thomas was resourceful and he told his young wife in their comfortable home in Miami not to worry.

Meanwhile, the previous spring, the owner of the Los Angeles Rams, Dan Reeves, had died at age fifty-eight of a lingering disease. For one season the team operated more or less in limbo under Reeves's capable old staff while the estate was being settled. It was common knowledge around the NFL that Reeves's heirs had little interest in football and wanted out.

Considering the capital involved—the going price for an expansion team is $16 million—pro football is not a wise investment. There are some tax advantages, but these are limited and shrinking with each legal decision and new law passed in Washington. The game has become an expensive hobby for men who have made their money elsewhere. They probably won't lose anything, but they won't make much, either. What they get is a place in the public eye and the right to associate with sweaty jocks. "Normal and successful people will get into this sport and then turn idiot," Rosenbloom once told Robert Boyle of *Sports Illustrated*.

Thomas, entering his fifties and with a young bride and daughter to provide for, surveyed the pro football scene. He knew Rosenbloom was unhappy, but Rozelle's public statements had trapped him in Baltimore. Rozelle would not allow the abandonment of a franchise that had been so well supported by the fans. Thomas also guessed that Rosenbloom was not about to sell out. The capital gains taxes would be enormous. Also CR was not a quitter and he loved the associations of pro football.

Thomas was aware, too, that Rosenbloom now owned a major share of a Hollywood movie studio, Warner Brothers, and lived most of the time in Los Angeles. CR liked the southern California life.

And the Rams were for sale.

A grandiose plan hatched in Thomas's fertile mind. He was about to embark on the greatest talent hunt of his career. He didn't seek a Tarkenton, an Eller, or a Page; a Csonka, a Warfield, or a Griese—or even someone who would become Bert Jones. What he sought was a millionaire with cash to spare and what, for want of a more delicate phrase, could be termed a terminal case of jock itch. A millionaire so anxious to join the pro football fraternity, to associate with such as George Halas and John Unitas, that he would turn

over his checkbook to Joe Thomas and be forever grateful
for the privilege.

Joe Thomas, who could remember his parents' struggle in
Warren, Ohio, and who had bristled under the direction of
such strong men as Jim Finks and Norm Van Brocklin in
Minnesota and Joe Robbie and Don Shula in Miami, would
have a fiefdom of his own.

Joe Thomas, as always, found his man.

Robert (Tiger) Irsay was a Chicago industrialist so nicknamed because he could never remember names or faces or
put them together, so he called everyone "Tiger." This would
not be a first in Baltimore. Babe Ruth, a native of that city,
called everyone "Kid" because of the same failing.

This is how the Colts' press guide describes Irsay:

". . . was raised in the rugged 'Bucktown' section of Chicago's north side and worked his way through school. At the
University of Illinois he made the team as a 'walk-on' . . .
[but] he eventually quit football because of his studies."

A marine in World War II, Irsay worked in the mechnical
contracting business until 1951 when, with the aid of $800 in
savings he said he borrowed from his wife, he formed a
heating and air conditioning firm. Twenty years later he sold
out for many millions. The transaction gave him the money
and the time. He had always admired the Colts and John
Unitas. He and George Halas were friends.

If Bob Irsay had not existed, Joe Thomas would have had
to invent him.

Irsay, though, was not Joe's first angel. For openers,
Thomas thought he had all the financial backing he needed
from Willard H. (Bud) Keland of Racine, Wisconsin, a
former minority owner of the Dolphins who had been forced
out of the Miami picture by Joe Robbie.

Keland thought he could use some partners and that's how

Irsay came into the picture. Thomas had known Keland through their early association with the Dolphins. He heard about Irsay from the doctor who had performed open heart surgery on him (Thomas) the previous winter. The doctor had a brother who was an attorney and who had done some work for this sports nut in Chicago named Irsay. Irsay had owned a small piece of the Montreal Expos in baseball and he wanted back in sports in the worst way.

As Keland began to experience problems in his cash flow, Irsay took over more and more of the deal until he had it 100 percent.

Once he found his financing, Thomas brought all the threads together to form a mind-boggling tapestry.

Irsay (outbidding a wealthy Jacksonville, Florida, attorney named Hugh Culverhouse, who later got the expansion Tampa Bay franchise) would buy the Rams from Reeves's heirs for $19 million, a record for an NFL franchise. He then would turn around and swap teams with Rosenbloom, assuming ownership of the Colts where Thomas would be placed in charge. A franchise in Los Angeles, of course, was worth much more than one in Baltimore, but this figured to be balanced out because the Colts supposedly had a large cash reserve and also were still owed $1.8 million of the $3 million they were to be paid for moving into the American Conference.

The transaction had tremendous advantages for Rosenbloom, not the least of which was the way it provided an escape route out of hostile Baltimore.

Most important, though, it enabled him to get out without paying a crippling capital gains tax. Remember, over the years he had laid out less than $2 million for total ownership of the Baltimore franchise.

Based on some estimates, Rosenbloom might have had to

pay more than $4 million in taxes in a 30 to 35 percent range if he had sold the Colts outright.

This was avoided.

In addition, by setting up a new corporation in Los Angeles, Rosenbloom could depreciate the Rams' players all over again. Depreciation of talent is a major source of sports tax advantage although currently under attack in court and Congress. Ball players in all sports can be depreciated just like trucks and typewriters. This is why when a new owner pays $16 million for an expansion football team most of the money is supposedly earmarked to pay for the veteran players he will receive from the established teams in an allocation draft. The higher the "book" value on these players, the greater the tax benefits as they are depreciated.

Players can only be depreciated once, unless the team is sold or moved to a new location under a different corporation. This is why Charles O. Finley moved his Athletics from Kansas City, where they had been well supported, to Oakland some years back.

When the flying decimals had settled, Rosenbloom had escaped Baltimore without damage and, in fact, with significant financial gain. Bitter Baltimoreans still remembered how he had started it all with a pledge of $13,000. Joe Thomas got a team to run and a position of what he thought was unassailable authority. And Tiger Irsay, who showed up on game days with a gang of friends to have a party like the rich fraternity kids who boozed it up at the stadium while he was working his way through Illinois, had his instant success symbol. Who before had ever heard of Robert Irsay, air conditioning tycoon?

In his first pronouncement, Irsay vowed to keep the Colts and John Unitas in Baltimore forever.

But one of the first things he discovered when he looked

over the books more closely was that Colts players owed the organization more than $600,000 as a result of personal loans from Rosenbloom, including more than $50,000 for game tickets.

Within months, Rosenbloom also had managed to spirit the Colts' team Super Bowl trophy out of Baltimore. Under the pretext that the NFL had scheduled a trophy "display" at the upcoming Super Bowl in Los Angeles, CR conned one of his old employees into sending the silver Tiffany showpiece out to the Rams. It turned out there was no "display" and the trophy has been seen in Rosenbloom's Bel-Air, California, mansion.

Thomas never made much of an issue over this because it wasn't "his" Super Bowl trophy and he figured he'd be winning plenty more on his own.

In addition, Irsay took over the NFL's highest payroll, averaging $31,000 a man; a commitment to train in Tampa and play three preseason games there; and, in Unitas, a thirty-nine-year-old quarterback with a history of arm trouble and assorted other ailments.

The Colts were starting training camp when Irsay and Thomas completed their coup, which meant there could be no changes in field direction of the team.

Don McCafferty, the Easy Rider, remained in charge, but in the worst kind of setting for his slack rein.

Because of Rosenbloom's desire to ingratiate himself with Tampa interests—and to show Baltimore politicians he was serious about a potential move—the Colts set up camp in that city. Now, there's nothing wrong with Tampa. It's a lovely place and parts of it can be suitably Spartan. But one of these parts was not the University of South Florida where the Colts were domiciled in a high-rise dorm on the attractive campus.

Even this might not have been so bad, but coeds also lived in the building, albeit on separate floors. It was not difficult for young, single Colts to find other matters than football with which to occupy themselves.

Close observers of the Colts insist that any chance this team had of making the play-offs was blown away in the congenial Gulf Coast breeze.

These were just symptoms, however. At the bottom line, Irsay and Thomas had inherited an aging, clubby ball club staffed with veterans of reputation but no future.

On the other hand, there was a pretty good draft list. The Colts had three picks on the second round. With the second of these choices they had selected Glenn Doughty, a tough receiver from Michigan, and with the third they tapped Lydell Mitchell, a feisty halfback from Penn State.

Doughty, who can turn a phrase, says he was destined to be a football player "from the day I came out the chute," meaning he was born to play. He played Little League ball in Detroit and later starred at Pershing High, a school most famous for some of its basketball alumni like Spencer Haywood, Ralph Simpson, and Mel Daniels. He chose Michigan because of its proximity and its academics and he attracted the pros even though the Wolverines seldom threw the ball.

He was tough and he could block and he had good hands. Maybe he got them from his father, an illustrative draftsman for the Post Office Department in Detroit. "It always amazed me how he could draw with such big hands," Doughty says. "His brush always looked like a toothpick but he would come out with the best paintings. He just had a fine touch."

Mitchell was from Salem, New Jersey, a smoke-shrouded industrial community in the southern part of the state not far from Wilmington, Delaware. His father worked in a factory and Lydell pointed himself toward pro football from the eighth grade on. "You know, I can tell you in five minutes how I got started playing football, but you're talking about twenty years," he mused one afternoon over lunch. "I'd like to know how many miles I've run. Not miles on the track, but just running plays; this one over and over, that one over and over."

Mitchell, like most running backs, is haunted by the specter of knee damage in that injury-prone position. He talks often of quitting while in one piece.

Mitchell was half of one of the great college backfields at Penn State. Franco Harris, now of the Steelers, was the fullback. Harris is also from southern New Jersey. The boys knew of each other because they were fighting for the scoring championship, but were not acquainted.

One day Joe Paterno, the Penn State coach, was passing over the area in a private plane on a recruiting trip. "You know, there are two guys down there I want to get and if I can get them we'll really do some things," he told Ernie Accorsi, then Penn State sports information director and now the Colts' assistant general manager.

One weekend, Mitchell was invited to visit the Penn State campus. Franco Harris was there, too. "I figured it was an accident, that he was just passing through, but it was really all planned. Funny how Joe finagled that," Mitchell says.

As Paterno had anticipated, the two became friends on that weekend visit and, in a sense, they may have ended up recruiting each other for Penn State. They're still close, too, and will show up to see each other play as pros when the schedule permits.

Also on that draft list masterminded by George Young were defensive back Bruce Laird and, on the seventeenth and last round, a smallish linebacker from Ohio State, Stan White.

All would be regulars during the great Baltimore turn-around.

Thomas's most significant deal this first year was consummated soon after the Colts started their preseason schedule. From what he saw in early camp, he was growing increasingly skeptical of Unitas as a man on whom to build his new version of the Colts. Morrall, of the same generation, had been released on waivers. Thomas felt he had to have a young quarterback on the grounds and Marty Domres, a three-year veteran, was available from the Chargers.

For sub tight end John Andrews and a first-round draft choice, Domres became a Baltimore Colt.

Domres was a member of a very exclusive NFL fraternity. He had played his college football in the Ivy League, at Columbia. Few Ivy Leaguers made it in the pros, but the quick-witted and glib Domres had been a standout in his collegiate competition and the Chargers made him their first-round selection in 1969. Only ten college players were chosen ahead of him. He was the perfect size—6-4, 222—and possessed an adequate arm, good running ability, and the intelligence to master an offense.

Less than two weeks after he joined the Colts, he took over for an injured Unitas and guided Baltimore to an exhibition victory over Kansas City.

With the acquisition of Domres, the lines of conflict were squarely drawn between Thomas and his lame duck coach, McCafferty.

McCafferty was loyal to the Colts who had won a Super Bowl for him, especially the legendary Unitas. Most coaches feel more comfortable with the known quantity, the player who will not make the unexpected mistake. By nature, they resist change, maybe because in football most changes involve firing the coach.

Thomas is the opposite. He is dean of the do-something-even-if-it's-wrong school. He chafed impatiently in the press box as he watched McCafferty ignore many of the rookies and other young players. He had not traded for Domres so the handsome Ivy Leaguer could sit in awe and watch Unitas play.

It took only five weeks, during which the Colts fell out of contention with four losses, all of them at home, for the break to come.

The Colts lost to Dallas, 21-0, on a Sunday with Unitas at quarterback. By the next day, McCafferty was out, with defensive line coach John Sandusky his "interim" replacement.

Unitas had some pretty good statistics for the first five games but he admits he had not played well against the Cowboys. He was beat up, too, so that Monday he drove to the stadium for treatment. En route, his car radio blared the news of McCafferty's firing.

Unitas was in the whirlpool when he was called to the phone.

According to the quarterback, the conversation went like this:

"John?"

"Yeah."

"This is Joe Thomas."

"Yeah."

"I guess you know we fired McCafferty."

"Yeah, I heard it on the radio."

"That means we're going to be playing the younger players a lot more."

"Fine."

"Okay." Click.

The young players had to mean those other guys, Unitas

must have thought to himself, but the next day he learned just what Thomas meant.

Sandusky called him into his bare office in the stadium, the room that so recently had belonged to McCafferty.

Again, the conversation is etched permanently in Unitas's memory, like a long-ago pass play that won a championship.

"I just want you to know that this is not my idea," the likable, heavy-set Sandusky opened what was obviously a painful conversation, "but I have been told by Joe Thomas that you are no longer to play another play with the Baltimore Colts."

"What do you mean?"

"It means Domres is starting from here on out."

"Just like that?"

"It's not me," Sandusky replied uncomfortably. "I'd rather have you in there, but it's orders from them."

Unitas, stung, grasped at his pride. "Okay," he said, "but, John, I'm not gonna run the clock out for you."

"I wouldn't do that to you," Sandusky, a former player himself, answered sympathetically.

Unitas offered to help Domres in any way he could, but this was pretty much meaningless. The two did not really get along. They came from different generations, different worlds.

Unitas recalls that he got into a game for only one play the rest of the season when Domres was stunned, threw a touchdown pass and came right out.

The handling of Unitas was Thomas's biggest blunder in running the Colts.

The quarterback was enraged at this brusque treatment after all those years and all the championships he had brought to Baltimore. He felt he deserved better, and he did. It was a complicated situation that caused damage to all concerned.

Unitas was not completely blameless. He refused to admit that at age thirty-nine he was a mere replica of the greatest quarterback of all time. His arm was gone, his legs were shot, and in any given season he figured to clock more time in the whirlpool convalescing than he did on the practice field.

Rosenbloom had known this. McCafferty knew it, too. Neither could bring himself to put it to Unitas. They lost their nerve in the face of this implacable legend.

Simply put, Unitas in a wheelchair would have tried to run over any man who told him he was through.

On the other hand, Unitas in civilian clothes still represented a tremendous asset to the Colts. Rosenbloom had recognized this and many years before signed the quarterback to a ten-year contract at $30,000 annually commencing the season after Unitas retired as a player. Unitas was supposed to work "full time" for the money but the understanding was that this wouldn't be a nine-to-five commitment. He was just to be on call when needed, presumably as a goodwill ambassador.

All Thomas had to do was wait a few Sundays until the Colts were mathematically eliminated from the championship race or until Unitas inevitably was injured. He then could have suggested, "What say we look at the kid?" Unitas would have sulked, but at least he would have been spared public embarrassment.

And he would have been saved for the franchise! The Colts from the beginning have engaged in almost continuous warfare with the city of Baltimore and with the Orioles over use of their stadium. It's one thing to have Joe Thomas or Bob Irsay go down to talk to the aldermen, quite another to have the team represented by the legendary John Unitas. The aldermen would have been too busy asking for autographs to vote against him.

In benching Unitas when and how he did, Thomas made

the right move in a football sense, the wrong move for the franchise.

Enraged, Unitas lashed out publicly at Thomas. "I will never be able to work for that man," Unitas said, referring to his postcareer contract. Thomas told him after the season to retire or be traded. Unitas thought he could still play and he became even more angry when George Allen of the Redskins told the quarterback he had tried to obtain his services in a trade after John had been benched during the season. Thomas denied it.

In a conversation in Los Angeles before the Super Bowl, Unitas said the question of a trade came up again. He said he asked only the courtesy of being informed about what teams were interested in him. "Then I'll tell you which ones I want to go to, if any, and you make the best deal you can," he offered.

According to Unitas, this was agreed upon.

Ten days later, Unitas had just arisen at his home in Towson, Maryland, just outside Baltimore, to catch a plane. He was speaking at a Quarterback Club dinner in Florida.

Larry Harris, one of Baltimore's football writers, was on the phone.

"What the hell you doing going to San Diego?" Harris demanded.

"What you talking about, I'm going to Florida," Unitas says he replied.

"Oh, no," Harris countered, "Joe Thomas just traded you to San Diego for $150,000."

"Well, that's the first I heard of it, but if you say so I believe it," Unitas said with a shrug and hung up.

Several minutes later, after checking through an intermediary whether Unitas would talk to him, Joe Thomas called and curtly informed the greatest quarterback in football history that he had been sold outright to the San Diego Chargers.

Unitas completed his career with little success or dignity in San Diego. He played in only five games for the Chargers in 1973 and then retired the following season in training camp after crossing a picket line of the striking NFL Players' Association so he would officially be marked present.

The bitterness continued as Unitas's career wound down. He and Thomas fought over the Rosenbloom contract. They went to the commissioner, they threatened to go to court. Unitas said he finally settled for $100,000, which still put the Colts $50,000 ahead considering the sale price from San Diego. Even today, Unitas says of Thomas, "He can't look you in the eye."

Thomas, for his part, ordered that Unitas be considered a nonperson in the Colts' office. All requests for pictures, autographs, appearances were to be referred to the old quarterback's Baltimore restaurant, the Golden Arm. It was as if the Jets would suddenly decide that Joe Namath had never played for them. A spiteful waste.

There is a postscript, however. When Thomas was deposed as general manager at the close of the 1976 season, one of the first moves of the new leadership was to heal the breach with Unitas. When the writer visited Baltimore to finish research for this book, the Unitas file was resurrected from its basement hiding place.

Back to the 1972 season of many Colts' discontent.

For game six, John Sandusky was on the sidelines as head coach and Marty Domres was the starting quarterback. The Colts ended up with a 5-9 record—4-5 under Sandusky—but they weren't that good. Four of the victories came over hapless division rivals New England and Buffalo and the fifth was a one-point upset over Cincinnati.

As the season progressed, Thomas ruthlessly cleaned house. By the start of the 1973 campaign, Bob Vogel had retired and the general manager had discarded such past stars as Unitas, Tom Matte, Dan Sullivan, Bill Curry, Bubba Smith, Fred Miller, Jerry Logan, Tom Nowatzke, Norm Bulaich, and—remember this name—Billy Newsome.

With each slice of the knife, the uproar increased, for Thomas very seldom was able to obtain live bodies or even top-rank draft choices for these oldsters. The remaining veterans reacted with bitter anguish as their old teammates and friends departed. They accused Thomas of raping the ball club for the gratification of his own ego. If he got rid of all the old stars, he could then take total credit for any future championships that might accrue. The veterans aired their gripes to friendly sports writers who took up the cry. Colt fans responded. Joe Thomas was wrecking a great team. He became the most unpopular man in town.

Professional sports are so successful in this country because the people need heroes. Thomas was defrocking Baltimore's legends before the public's very eyes. Only two years earlier these same players had won a Super Bowl. What on earth was going on?

Few noted that most of the veterans he cut loose failed to hook on with other teams. Those that did failed to distinguish themselves.

The turmoil of a team in transition made life especially difficult for young players on the Colts, the ones Thomas was pushing. Players resent rookies who come along to take the jobs of their old friends. The resentment is fanned when all the veterans find themselves vulnerable.

Glenn Doughty recalls his first season as a professional: "It was hell.

"It was like you were on the outside of an empire," he

remembers. "They just ignored you, they didn't want to talk to you; they looked down their nose at you because you were a rookie. A lot of guys would have said, 'Well, this is crazy; this is madness,' but it's only because of my competitiveness and the toughness of [coach] Bo Schembechler and Michigan that I'm here now."

It required tremendous self-discipline for Doughty just to cope with Unitas.

"When I came here it was like Unitas could walk on water and after all these years of watching on TV, well, all of a sudden I'm catching passes from No. 19 and that's a mind-blower in itself," Doughty said. "Before long, though, you realize that he's not the Unitas of old and then you've got to say that's something he has to deal with. This is my job, my livelihood and I've got to improve myself, even though his ball is wobbly and not as accurate as I had anticipated."

Doughty sensed other bad vibrations. Because he was late arriving after the All-Star game, he felt the coaches overloaded him with new pass patterns so he could catch up. And then, every once in a while, it seemed Unitas would call a pattern that Doughty hadn't been taught. "A lot of psychological things were going down and when he did this to mess with me, it made me look bad. I'd run the wrong pattern because it hadn't been put in that week and I'd get yelled at," Doughty remembers.

Rookies were not welcomed in this closed Colts society, articulate black rookies least of all. Those who survived had to be good and they had to be tough and, as Doughty says with some satisfaction, "It was just a matter of time but I dealt with it, and after a couple of years those people were on the outside looking in."

Despite his personal popularity and near-break-even record, Sandusky was not retained as head coach. Thomas cast about for a new man. There is always a rush to sign assistants off a championship team and at this point aides on the Miami staff were most in demand.

Don Shula, once rapped by Rosenbloom for his alleged failures to "win the big one"—and then called "piggish" by his old boss when he jumped to Miami for more money and responsibility—had just carried his Dolphins through the Super Bowl for a perfect 17-0 record. Ironically, that final victory in Super VII was played in Los Angeles, Carroll Rosenbloom's new home base. At his victory press conference, Shula expressed extra satisfaction that he had won the big one "in this particular city."

Thomas first offered the Colts job to Bill Arnsparger, Shula's top defensive aide, but was turned down. Then he turned to Charley Winner, former head coach of the St. Louis Cardinals and at that time an assistant in Washington. Winner also declined.

Finally, Thomas was able to hire Howard Schnellenberger, the man who ran Shula's offense at Miami.

All this time, Thomas also was scouting college talent, his real forte. He haunted the camps of the various all-star teams, especially the two Senior Bowl squads preparing to play in Mobile, Alabama. This is the premier all-star game, with participants chosen mainly for their pro potential. "You get to see the best against the best," scouts say, and they are welcomed to the practice fields.

All autumn, Thomas had been getting reports about an emerging senior quarterback at Louisiana State named Bert Jones. Thomas had known Dub Jones for years, in fact had once hired him as a part-time scout for the Dolphins.

Bert had a big game in the Senior Bowl despite being hampered all week by a serious attack of the flu, and by now everybody knew about Dub's boy. "As fine a quarterback as

any of the ones available in recent years," Thomas declared,
and he knew he was understating.

The problem for Thomas was how to get a shot at this
bayou prodigy. The Colts had tenth pick in the upcoming
college draft and Bert would be gone long before then.
Houston, with the worst record in football, got to lead off.

As time drew closer for the late January draft, the Oilers
were besieged with phone calls offering trades for that
prized position. "We're only accepting calls that are pre-
paid," laughed John Breen, their personable general manager.

No less than eleven teams called to make offers. It was
reminiscent of the pressure New England faced for the right
to draft Jim Plunkett or the dozens of calls Pittsburgh received the year Terry Bradshaw was available.

The temptations to a losing team are great. The Oilers
were 1-and-13 in 1972 and they needed help up and down
the line. Rich teams offered them four or five instant regulars, players who might provide immediate respectability.

But the Oilers stood firm with a stronger bargaining
stance than most teams in their position. They already
owned two fine quarterbacks in Dan Pastorini and Lynn
Dickey. They could trade off that first draft pick, they could
draft Jones and then trade him or one of their other quarterbacks, or they could go a different route altogether by keeping the lead-off pick and choosing someone else.

Thomas soon realized that the pressure was too strong on
Houston. Balitmore, still building, could not afford this auction. Instead, Thomas took a different tack. He decided to
approach the New Orleans Saints, who chose second and
already owned a promising young quarterback in Archie
Manning.

The Saints had a former astronaut, Dick Gordon, running

their football team. In the context of what developed, this is all you had to know.

"What would you want for your first-round choice in the draft?" Thomas asked by phone one day as if making idle conversation.

Thomas knew the Saints needed defensive linemen and he was prepared to go high. Even though Bubba Smith had torn up his knee in a freak accident in preseason when he ran into a sideline marker, the monstrous lineman was still a very highly regarded property. But he was a headache to Thomas, who also doubted whether Smith would make it all the way back from surgery. He had once threatened Bubba with a large fine if he didn't leave the sidelines during a Colts game. As usual, Thomas was right but as usual he was undiplomatic. On the sidelines in a heavy cast after his operation, Bubba could not have moved out of the way if a play came in his direction. But Joe could have taken a minute to point it out to him. Bubba, trying to show team spirit, was hurt. Later Thomas threatened to fine Smith $100 every day he missed his postoperative rehab session.

Thomas was ready to surrender Bubba, and more, for the Saints' selection.

Gordon wasn't ready to take this bait, however. He was too shrewd. "We would want," he said, "Billy Newsome."

Thomas, perhaps for the first time in his life, was stunned. Newsome was a journeyman defensive lineman just completing his third season. He had been no better than a fifth-round draft choice out of Grambling College and had done little since to project as a future all-pro. "Quietest man on the team," read the Baltimore press guide and that about summed up Billy Newsome. Defensive linemen are supposed to be exuberant, loud, and aggressive.

Thomas was not only nonplussed, he was speechless. He

Bert's concentration shows in action against the Dolphins.

Bert Jones scores against Notre Dame in the game that established him finally as LSU's No. 1 quarterback.

Bert passing through the fog in his greatest pro victory against Miami.

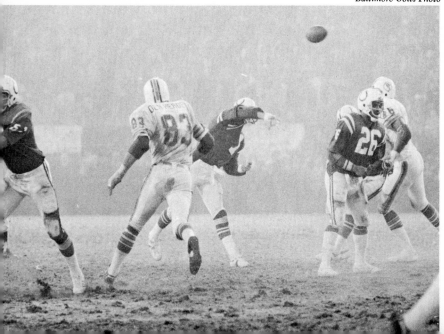

Bert Jones, the serious college quarterback.

Dub Jones, Bert's daddy, on the day he scored six touchdowns against Chicago for the Cleveland Browns, November 25, 1951.

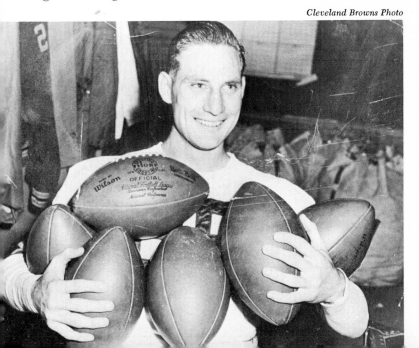

Alan Ameche scoring the biggest touchdown in Colts' history as the Colts beat the Giants in overtime for the 1958 NFL championship.

Two Colts eras overlap when GM Joe Thomas (left) presents a commemoratory plaque to Weeb Ewbank, making his last trip to Baltimore before retiring as head coach of the Jets.

Carroll Rosenbloom, intense master of the franchise.

Tension finally shows as Jim O'Brien answers questions following his winning Super Bowl field goal.

Raymond Berry, who made himself a Hall of Famer.

Gene (Big Daddy) Lipscomb, a Baltimore legend.

Both photos: Baltimore Colts Photo

Lenny Moore, danger on the gridiron.

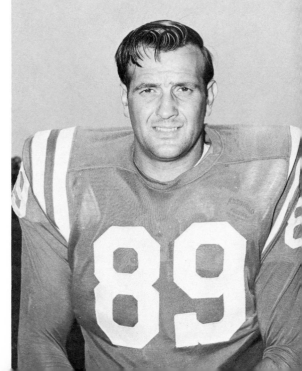

Gino Marchetti. All they could do was applaud.

Both photos: Baltimore Colts Photo

The quarterback greats of their era, Bart Starr (left) and John Unitas.

Right: The great draft of 1955. Top choices, in order, were quarterback George Shaw, fullback Alan Ameche and center Dick Szymanski. Two decades later, Szymanski was named general manager.

Above: Mike Curtis, who played it his way.

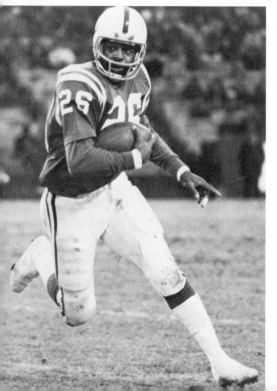

Left: Lydell Mitchell, from the bad days to the playoffs.

Stan White getting the drop on pass defense.

John Dutton shedding blockers against the Bears.

Both photos: Baltimore Colts Photo

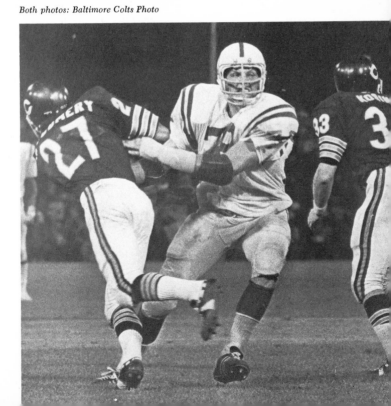

George Kunz appears a bemused bystander on sidelines, but it's only pre-season.

Both photos: Baltimore Colts Photo

Roger Carr takes an oxygen break during one of the Colts' track-meet victories over the Jets.

Bert Jones demonstrates his unique over-the-top passing motion despite Redskins' rush.

Glenn (Shake and Bake) Doughty holds court on picture day.

Joe Ehrmann's mind is on the game, not on Colts' next party at this point.

Both photos: Baltimore Colts Photo

Into each superstar's life a little Pete Barnes (of the Patriots) must fall.

Bert Jones, as always, is in command.

stalled for time. "Uh, I'll call you right back," he told the astronaut. He still wasn't sure he had heard correctly.

Minutes later, Thomas was back on the phone. "You say you want Billy Newsome?" he repeated. The astronaut confirmed his original request, but asked for another draft choice as well. Thomas magnanimously threw in a fourth. Later on he would deal Bubba Smith to Oakland for a superb tight end, Raymond Chester.

Completing the trade with New Orleans didn't assure the Colts of a shot at Bert Jones, but at least they now had a realistic chance. And if they didn't get Bert, they could replace Newsome with one of the two blue chip defensive linemen available that year, John Matuszak of Tampa and Dave Butz of Purdue, each 6 foot 7, 275—and destined to become the biggest first-round flops in draft history. But nobody knew this at the time.

Draft day loomed three days after the trade with New Orleans and now everything depended on Houston. At 10:00 A.M. in New York's modern Americana Hotel, Commissioner Pete Rozelle stepped to the microphone in the crowded ballroom to announce the opening selections, a ceremonial he enjoys.

In the first two rounds, each team has fifteen minutes to exercise its choice and five minutes thereafter. The Oilers were called. For almost twelve minutes their representative in the ballroom sat embarrassed at the end of an open telephone line. The Oilers obviously were weighing last-minute offers or, perhaps, simply hoping that someone would call with a new proposal they couldn't refuse.

Finally, the Houston representative leaned over his little three-by-five card and printed a name, a position, and a school. An aide from the league office carried the card to Rozelle, who intoned through his microphone in formal tones for the television cameras, "Houston selects John Matuszak, defensive tackle, from Tampa."

Only a few minutes earlier, Marty Domres had strolled into the room. The personable Columbia kid was in good spirits as he greeted old friends from the New York press, writers who had covered him during his college days at Columbia. For the first time he could return to the scene of his collegiate triumphs as a bona fide professional quarterback. He was glib and expansive. Joe Thomas had called him the Colts' quarterback of the future. They had benched John Unitas just so he could play.

Mere seconds after Houston's selection of Matuszak, Domres's smile froze. Rozelle relayed the Baltimore pick: "Bert Jones, quarterback, LSU."

Thomas's maneuvering had paid off. "When you have the opportunity to get a quarterback of his stature, you have to take him. He is everything you want in a quarterback, the finest quarterback prospect I have ever seen come out of college football," Thomas raved, "the kind of quarterback who can make a franchise."

If Domres was surprised by this turn of events, Jones was not. His father had remained close to professional football even after he left the Browns. He knew coaches and he knew scouts and he knew his son was rated highly, and by whom.

So forewarned, Bert knew he would be a top choice and as draft time approached he learned from his father which teams were trying to deal with Houston for that lead-off position so they could draft him. He knew Baltimore had made a strong bid but had been turned down. Being at LSU, he of course was aware of the Colts' trade with New Orleans only days before the draft.

Dub and Bert could think along with Thomas, but the great imponderable was Houston, always an erratic organization. Would the Oilers draft Bert as chattel for a subsequent trade?

It was about quarter after nine in the morning, Louisiana time, that Bert Jones got his answer. He had been drafted No. 1 by the Baltimore Colts.

After talking to Joe Thomas, Bert had time to reflect on some daydreaming he had done a year earlier as a junior in college.

"You know how everyone does their 'wishes'?" he recalled some years later. "Well, I kind of sat down and wondered what teams needed quarterbacks. I said to myself, 'Well, John is getting old and Earl is getting old and Baltimore would really be the place to play.' It's pretty ironic that this is where I ended up, isn't it?"

7
In Touch With Reality

▬

There were two tasks awaiting Bert Jones before he could qualify to don the Colts' traditional white helmet with its familiar blue horseshoe decals.

He had to sign his contract and he had to fulfill a commitment to play in the College All-Star game in Chicago against the defending world champion Dolphins.

The contract posed little problem, even though Bert was in a position to ask for the moon and a percentage of all crab cake sales in Baltimore for the duration of his career.

The element of greed does not appear in Bert's psychological profile, and negotiations went smoothly. The quarterback did not hire an agent but instead was represented by his father. "If my father doesn't know, who does?" Bert asked, but just to make sure he wasn't negotiating for 1950-style numbers, Dub called his old boss, Paul Brown. Brown, by now coach and major domo of the Cincinnati Bengals, filled Dub in on the kind of money and fringes first-round draft choices were getting these days.

A family friend who was an attorney looked over the papers for loopholes and, for more money than Dub had collected in his entire pro career, Bert Jones became a Baltimore Colt. The estimated figures are $50,000 signing bonus and escalating annual salaries of $35,000, $45,000 and $60,000.

That spring the Colts brought Bert in for a weekend. They asked Glenn Doughty to come out and catch some balls and Doughty was impressed. "He could throw the ball, there wasn't any doubt about that," Doughty said after their solitary workout.

The College All-Star game, discontinued after the 1976 edition because of rising costs, was always approached with mixed emotions by the young professionals. They usually lost the game to the more cohesive and experienced Super Bowl champions, but that was secondary to the three precious weeks of training camp they missed while drilling in Chicago. Many marginal players lost whatever chance they may have had for a pro career because of this late start. Others, who suffered injuries in practice or in the game, blew a whole season—or career.

For others, though, playing in the All-Star game remains a thrilling memory. Doughty, for instance, says there was no way he would have allowed the Colts to talk him out of playing. Associations formed at the All-Star game stay with a player for years and few ever forget the chill they felt when the spotlight hit as they ran through the goalposts to be introduced at historic Soldier Field.

Bert chafed at the time he had to spend working out at Northwestern University near Chicago when he could have been with the Colts. "I'm at the end of my rope. This has been the longest three weeks of my life," he told visiting Phil Jackman of the Baltimore Sun. "I should be where I'm going to be from now on—but I'll catch up."

The experience wasn't totally negative for Bert, however, and actually included some satisfying moments. He was reminded that his father had played in this same game in 1946 when the collegians beat the Rams, 16-0, and he also had to feel pretty good inside when the starting elevens were posted. Bert would open at quarterback for the All-Stars. His backup? None other than Joe Ferguson of Arkansas, the man who had been Mr. Everything when they graduated from high school. Ferguson had been drafted down in the third round by Buffalo.

Back at Towson State College near Baltimore, most of the Colts were gathered around television sets to watch the game. They had a clinical interest in the Dolphins, their division rivals whom they would play twice in regular season. And they also wanted to get a preview of their No. 1 draft choice, Bert Jones, plus two other Colt prospects, fullback Bill Olds and linebacker Jamie Rotella. Both had been third-round draft choices. Players in their respective positions watched more closely than the others.

Domres, known as one of the Colts' premier needlers and practical jokers, had experienced a particularly rough time in recent days. His teammates knew how shocked he had been when the Colts drafted Jones and they showed no mercy. "Boy, we hear that kid's really been throwing the ball in Chicago," Stan White jibed at Domres across the line of scrimmage during practice. "Yeah, but that linebacker's looking pretty good, too," Domres shot back. All the Colts liked Domres. He could dish it out, but he could take it, too.

Many of the veterans had played in the All-Star game as their introduction to pro football, so watching the rookies provided a frame of reference. "It was something we all could identify with and when you see a guy who's on your team play in it, you want to see how he does. Can he help us when he comes in?" Lydell Mitchell explained.

The All-Stars lost the game, 21-3, but few people connected with the Colts had any reason to regret Baltimore's choice of Bert Jones. Three times he led the All-Stars into scoring position inside the Dolphin's fifteen-yard line. Once he scrambled into the end zone on a broken play only to have the apparent touchdown nullified by a penalty. Teammates' errors canceled the other scoring chances.

Jones completed nine of seventeen passes for seventy-nine yards and Don Shula, the winning coach, was impressed. Shula especially liked the way Bert threw the dangerous and difficult sideline pass. "That ball didn't take very long to get out there," Shula declared.

Jones also made important points with his teammates. "We couldn't wait for him to show up," Mitchell recalls.

Still, no matter how good a kid looks on TV or even live in another context, the tell on a professional comes when he joins his teammates. Players don't trust write-ups.

"You hear so much," White explains. "You hear a guy is going to be another Johnny Unitas or Dick Butkus or Jim Parker, or whatever, and when you see them you're so disappointed. Most of the time they don't even live up to the requirements of a basic football player. You get so the more you hear the less you expect."

With just a trace of satisfaction, Stan White points out that the Colts' All-Star linebacker, Rotella, didn't even make the squad.

But Bert was different. He had the goods. The other veterans felt for Domres. "I don't think Marty expected Bert to be that good," White says sympathetically.

Jones arrived in Baltimore in time for a morning workout with his new team. That night the Colts had a public scrimmage scheduled at Towson. Bert didn't play, but he attracted plenty of attention from fans and players alike as he warmed up beforehand with the other quarterbacks. The

Colts marveled at his unique overhand delivery and the zip he put on his passes. Even his longest throws traveled straight on a line.

That night, Bert went out for a late dinner with some of the veterans. Fans in the restaurant recognized him immediately. He was an instant celebrity. But he sat quietly and his major conversational contribution was to tell the veterans about some of their old college teammates who had been in Chicago.

In these first days at Towson, Bert received the biggest dividend from those years spent as a ball boy with the Browns.

To most rookies, life in a pro camp is a mystery. Most admit that their biggest initial fear is not inability to perform, but worry that they will somehow mess up off the field and look foolish.

"I knew the hours, I knew the workouts. There was no startle to it," Bert says.

It also helped that the Colts were essentially a very young team, thanks to Thomas's ruthless pruning. Few of the "veterans" were much older than Bert. They remember Jones as a cocky kid from the day he first showed up. They use the word often. Bert had confidence in his skills but the veterans could see that it was not misplaced and so they accepted it. "He had his fundamentals down and he knew how to play the game," says Lydell Mitchell. "It was safe to say he had an awful lot of ability, and not just raw ability. He only needed experience, like everyone else."

Jones was not the only standout rookie with the Colts that year. Thanks to all his trades, Thomas had amassed seven picks in the first four rounds of the draft. After tabbing Jones, he used Baltimore's own first-round choice to select Joe Ehrmann, a free-spirited defensive tackle out of

Syracuse. And in round two he snatched Mike Barnes, a defensive lineman from the University of Miami. Barnes was somewhat of a sleeper because he had missed most of his junior year due to illness.

These first three Baltimore selections were not happenstance. To Thomas, you build a football team from two positions, the quarterback on offense and the front four on defense. Most ball clubs know this; few have the discipline to follow through.

Of his four selections in the next two rounds, Thomas was able to get some service only out of Olds, the running back. But then, in round five, he tabbed David Taylor, an offensive tackle from North Carolina's small Catawba College where he had set school records in the shot put and discus. Taylor would soon be a fixture in the starting lineup.

Despite his late start in training camp, Jones quickly was challenging Domres for the starting quarterback job. The other Colts watched with great interest. Domres had guile and experience. "One of the best field generals I've ever come across," says Doughty. Jones had sheer talent.

The Colts lost their first two preseason games under new coach Howard Schnellenberger with Domres at the helm. But in game three Jones came off the bench to direct two long scoring drives in a come-from-behind 32-28 victory over Detroit. His passing log was a phenomenal 11 for 15.

Two more defeats followed, but in the preseason finale against Denver, Jones again was brilliant with twelve completions in nineteen attempts for 130 yards and a touchdown as Baltimore won, 17-10.

As the Colts approached their season opener against Cleveland, Schnellenberger, the rookie coach, had to make his decision. Domres had experience, Jones had promise, and the new boy had been responsible for both exhibition victories. Too, he had come strong in the final game.

Schnellenberger elected to go with the kid. He would start Jones in the opener in Cleveland.

In fantasyland, Bert Jones would have to be the star in this return to the stadium where he had once shagged punts for the veteran who was now his teammate, David Lee. He would make them proud in Cleveland, where fans still remembered his daddy and where some of the Browns' old functionaries still recalled the quiet and respectful bucktoothed lad who was Dub's son.

But, alas, in sports there is always another team with fantasies of its own to live out. Many of the Browns' defensive linemen probably had drifted off to sleep the night before dreaming of how many quarterbacks they were going to tackle. In football, fantasies generally prevail only for the better players.

Bert Jones was sacked five times and intercepted once as he completed only six of twenty-two passes in a 24-14 loss. Glenn Doughty remembers one typical play: "Our pass protection had broken down and I happened to be looking back after I came out of my pattern. Walter Johnson had hold of Bert's head and, like, his shoulders were facing this way and his head was facing thataway, like it was on a swivel. That was what Bert was going through. That was what the whole team was going through."

A week later, Bert made his debut in Baltimore and threw four interceptions. Domres added four more in relief for a team record eight and the Colts lost to the Jets, 34-10.

Jones and the Colts finally got on the winning side in game three, but their victim was the perennially hapless New Orleans Saints and Bert's passing was incidental in the 14-10 victory. For the first time in seventeen years, Baltimore got twin 100-yard efforts from two running backs, Lydell Mitchell and Don McCauley. The Colts got all their points in the first quarter, then barely hung on as Bert threw four more interceptions. He had nine in three games.

That victory did give the rookie a reprieve, however. Schnellenberger decided to stay with him through losses to New England and Buffalo. In both games the Colts failed to score a touchdown until the fourth quarter when the issue was already decided. Bert was harassed and his interceptions mounted. Only his ability to turn poor pass protection into an occasional running gain kept him alive, but barely.

"I was literally being beaten to death," he recalls today.

However, despite the team's poor record and his own unimpressive statistics, Bert was totally unprepared when Schnellenberger informed him that Domres was going to take over as number one quarterback for the sixth game. And take over Domres did, completely. The Colts had nine games to play and Jones would see spot duty in only two of these. He did not get off the bench for a single offensive play for the last five games of his rookie season.

The Colts' decision was a logical one. Years ago, Norman Snead was considered one of the best quarterback prospects ever to come out of college. The Redskins, who had drafted him, made Snead their number one quarterback from the first week. At that time they were less than respectable, they were awful. Snead took a terrible weekly pounding. He became gun-shy and never really recovered to achieve even a small measure of his college potential.

Many years later, Terry Bradshaw enjoyed a rookie exhibition debut much the same as Bert's. Playing pro football was like picking cherries, he decided, unaware that most solid teams do not use their more sophisticated coverages in these games. Worse, Bradshaw commented publicly about how easy it was. The regular season became a nightmare of sacks, losses, and interceptions. By the time he was mercifully benched, Bradshaw had become a physical and emotional wreck. It took him years to recover.

The Colts wanted nothing like this to happen to Bert.

Jones still looks back at this episode with mixed feelings.

"I knew I had a good preseason, but then it was a combination of things. We were not as talented as the other teams and I myself was not as groomed as you might want a quarterback to be. The decision was made to keep me from being thrown to the dogs, from being beat on and beat on and beat on until you get scared," he concedes.

What probably riled Bert most was being dropped to the status of a virtual nonplayer for the last half of the season. But Schnellenberger had little choice here. Many of the veterans liked and admired Domres as a quarterback. To alternate both would have created a bad schism on the team and made things worse.

Still, Bert today adds stubbornly, "I don't question the coach's decision, but I felt then as I feel now, I wish I'd played."

Bert's problems were not strictly confined to the playing field. He was homesick and he felt stifled in Baltimore.

"How do I feel about Baltimore?" he repeats. "Well, Baltimore is a city and my initial reaction to any city is 'Where's the country?' To me Baltimore was strictly a place to play ball."

While growing up in Ruston, Bert had become not only a ball player, but a total outdoor person. As he says, "I love playing football, but if I could make my living hunting and fishing, that's what I'd do."

Hunting and fishing around Ruston provided the main outlets when Bert was growing up. "I can never remember not being able to walk out of the house and go hunting—for quail, rabbit, turkey, squirrel, deer, practically everything there is to hunt," he says. Later he expanded his interests to other outdoor activities. He took up scuba diving while still in college. Charley McClendon, his coach at LSU, didn't much like the idea, but there was little he could do. Even then Jones had the independent mind that set him apart from most of his peers. McClendon grudgingly accepted Bert's new pastime but told the quarterback's instructor, "When Jones dives, you dive with him."

Later, Bert would go diving in such exotic spots as British Honduras and occasionally he has found himself nose-to-nose with hammerhead sharks or barracuda. With no offensive line to help him here, he takes off on some really desperate scrambles.

Water skiing soon was added to his repertoire and then snow skiing, two more endeavors calculated to bring gray hairs to coaches who depended on his good health for their good fortune.

Eventually, Bert discovered it was taking him hours and hours to get to these various sporting sites. There also was the little matter of a five-hour drive each way to visit his girl friend, Danni Dupuis, on their increasingly frequent dates. So he bought an airplane and learned to fly it. More worry lines for Joe Thomas, et al.

As he began to settle in around Baltimore, Jones became acquainted with some Colts fans, Howard Meredith and Ed Boyd, who owned good hunting land on Maryland's Eastern Shore, about an hour's drive from his suburban apartment.

On Tuesdays, the Colts' normal day off, Bert sets his alarm so he can be ready to leave at four in the morning. It is dark outside, the weather is chill, even early in the season. Bert has told his coach after their film session the previous day that he is going hunting. "If you need me, I'll be back dark, an hour," he says. That means they will hunt until dark and he'll be home an hour after that.

He loads his shotguns, hunting hat, and camouflage suit and boots into his camper. There are small boxes of shells and extra camouflage paint. The jump suit probably won't be washed until after Bert gets home but there is something clean and comforting about the cumulative odor. It is the smell of the outdoors.

When Bert catalogues his equipment, it is always "my guns, my hat, my suit," etc. The things are important to him. These excursions are "my touch with reality."

Teammates have been alerted that Bert is going hunting and those that want to join him are welcome. Some know the way and meet him there. Others show up at the apartment to hitch a ride. Bert likes their company, but he is not dependent on it. "I'm going," he says simply. "It's up to them if they want to come with me—and they better be ready on time."

Robert Pratt, Bert's roommate on road trips and an offensive guard, is the most frequent hunting companion. He came along a year after Jones in the same rookie class as Bob Van Dyne, another lineman who often joins the safari. Both were extremely shy when they joined the Colts. Going hunting with the quarterback helped them to feel they belonged and brought them out of their shell. Veterans like Elmer Collett, George Kunz, and Forrest Blue also go along quite often. They are offensive linemen, too.

This, of course, is more than coincidence. No, there is nothing in their contracts that requires them to guard Jones from harm on their days off, too. But offensive linemen tend to be stolid, passive, patient types. It is hard to imagine a linebacker like Mike Curtis or a defensive lineman like Joe Ehrmann sitting for hours in a duck blind waiting for his quarry to fly into range, which is pretty much the philosophy of pass blocking. Defensive players are search-and-destroy types. They seek out their targets.

Bert is the group leader, the guide, the instructor. He exults as his friends learn to share his joy.

George Kunz, a quiet giant who plays tackle, is one whom Jones has initiated into the outdoor fraternity. Now Kunz carries the message. "It's just the fact that you're outdoors," he said one day. "Watching dogs play in the woods, seeing a fox sneak up on a rabbit; these are things you don't get a chance to see anyplace else. Out there, Bert acts like he's back home in Ruston, Louisiana. He's like a kid when he puts on his boots and his hunting outfit, his hat.

"Bert really enjoys it and he likes to see his teammates enjoy it. He gets a kick out of seeing a teammate down his first duck, the whole idea of producing meat for the table.

"Bert enjoys watching other people enjoy and that's a very healthy attitude."

Within minutes of their departure, Bert has left the city and its suburbs behind and is speeding through the picturesque Maryland countryside as dawn slowly turns the darkness gray.

They arrive in time for a light breakfast with Ed and Howard and then it's out to the blinds. There will be plenty of time for a big hunter's breakfast about 9:00 or 10:00 A.M. Ducks and geese, these usually are in season when Bert is in Baltimore.

"The ducks usually start flying early, but it depends on the day and the weather," Bert explains. "It depends on the moon, too, and you have to kind of guesstimate what they're going to do and try to meet them halfway. If they always came at the same time, why you could just go out and wait for them, couldn't you?"

This is where Bert reveals the competitive aspects of the

outdoors, recalling the young boy in Ruston who "attacked" his games when the others were merely playing. Life outdoors—whether flying a plane, skiing a mountain, facing down a shark, or stalking the wild goose, all of which he does well—is a matter of competition, a challenge to be overcome. Like football.

When preparing to bag a goose for his dinner, Bert must prepare a game plan. What weapons to take along, where to lie in wait, when to be there. Like deciding what pass patterns will work best on Sunday and choosing the right time to use them.

"There's a feeling of accomplishment to bringing them in," Jones says of his hunting excursions. He speaks haltingly. These feelings have not been articulated before. They are just there, as the outdoors is just there.

"There is an air of competition, whatever it is drives a person," he continues. "I don't shoot [just] to kill. I stop at limits. I obey the law. In fact, I enjoy shooting my camera as much as I enjoy shooting my gun.

"There's just a feeling of being outdoors and I guess I can correlate it to sports in a sense. You're establishing your individuality. Most people can't do something like this and by doing it you accomplish something that other people can't accomplish. I enjoy it all, all the outdoors—scuba diving, skiing, hunting, whatever. I can't stand just to sit and watch television. I am not programmed to be a city person."

Flying his own plane is "another challenge" for Jones, but this is one of the areas where Bert, who appears to be the Huck Finn of football, shows that there is quite another side to his personality.

A country boy he is. A rube he is not.

You can sit in his apartment and listen to Willie Nelson country and western tunes on the stereo while Bert shows

slides of hunting scenes on his dining room wall and decline
to join the quarterback as he dips snuff or chews tobacco.
But moments later, Bert will spit tobacco juice into a water
glass and then get up and ask his visitor to share in a bottle
of French wine his neighborhood supplier has suggested.
A shipment has just come in, this vintage has just the right
bouquet. Bert has bought a case.

Take his airplane, appropriately registered as "7BJ."

"I know it sounds like an extravagance, but it's not. I
bought it pretty cheap. During the season when I'm up
here, I have it leased out. And I bought it with borrowed
money so a lot of the cost is tax-deductible interest. I know
flying is dangerous and that's why I'm very careful," he
explains.

Boy businessman, that's Bert. Sure he skis a lot in Aspen,
Colorado, but until recently he also owned part of a restaurant there. He owns apartment complexes, a timber farm,
and some years more than 1,000 acres in soy beans. He buys
and sells real estate. He runs cows on a farm he owns. Farm-
ing is what he thinks about getting into after football, although it undoubtedly would be more as an entrepreneur
than down in the dirt.

Not even counting his greatest asset, that strong right
arm, some estimate that Bert already is worth a million
dollars.

Put together, Bert Jones emerges as a precociously well-
rounded young man even if he seems constitutionally unable
ever to just relax and let life wash over him for a few peace-
ful moments. As Ted Marchibroda puts it, "Bert lives life to
the fullest, and plays football the same way."

By the end of his rookie season, Bert had reason to doubt
himself and his football future. It had been a discouraging
year, starting with such high hopes and ending with that

five-game sentence on the bench. Even during those unhappy semesters at LSU, Bert had never been shackled to the sidelines, a complete nonparticipant.

The Colts closed their 4-10 season with two straight victories in which Domres went all the way.

After the final game, which was played in Baltimore, Bert dressed quickly and sought out one of the Colts' assistant coaches, Pete McCulley. McCulley was Baltimore's receiver coach and in that capacity worked closely with the quarterbacks in framing the passing game plan each week.

McCulley and the Jones family had been friends for years. Pete had played his college football as a quarterback at Louisiana Tech before Bradshaw and later, as an assistant coach at Baylor, he had tried to recruit Bert out of high school.

He and Bert talked the same language.

"Pete had always been a good helping hand and he knew I was down and depressed," Bert says as he recalls that mid-December meeting in the Colts' shabby quarters beneath Memorial Stadium. "There was no doubt that at the time I felt I was better than Marty and he knew that. He also knew that this was probably the longest I had ever been away from home."

The two Louisiana home boys talked for a while. McCulley told Bert the technical areas in which he would have to improve to become a successful pro quarterback. "I know this was a low point for him," McCulley remembers, "but he left with the idea that he was just going to work harder. I suggested it, but he was more than willing. He showed some determination that he wasn't going to surrender easily."

Looking back, Bert says the post-game meeting "was something that helped keep me going."

"Keep your dauber up. Next year is gonna be different,"

McCulley told the young quarterback as they parted, but not before the two had made a date to get together in the off-season for a brief refresher course on football fundamentals, and confidence.

Bert's camper was fully loaded and waiting in the stadium parking lot for a quick departure back home. He needed to return to his roots, to restore his confidence and refresh his soul by tramping the fields he loved and drawing from his family and friends.

"I think I'll always be homebound, I'll always go back to Louisiana to my old friends for the huntin' and fishin'," Bert says.

Bert's dream is to return to the land, to farm near Ruston when his playing days are over. He is aware, of course, that the dream may not come true. In ten years or more of playing, he may outgrow the farm or be deflected by circumstances in other directions.

But even if it's only symbolically in his imagination, you know Bert means it when he says, "I'll always have that trailer packed before the last game."

8
No Freedom, No Football

This couldn't be professional football. This was Berkeley in the sixties, Detroit auto plants in the thirties. Angry men on picket lines, the threat of violence heavy on a hot summer day. Strike. National Football League players were on strike. Their symbol: a clenched fist. Their slogan: "No freedom, no football!"

The players' collective bargaining agreement with the owners had expired in January. In March negotiations began between the NFL Management Council, made up of the owners, and the Players' Association. There was no real bargaining. Harsh words were exchanged, positions polarized. The owners refused to make their annual payment into the pension fund. The players girded for a strike.

Money was a secondary issue. The players wanted a voice in their destiny. From the day he was drafted, a player was owned in perpetuity by the drafting team even if he never signed a contract or elected to play in Canada or formed his own league in Luxembourg. He had the right to "play out his option" and become a free agent, but even this was illusory. The signing team had to compensate his former club because of a league bylaw known as the "Rozelle Rule." Except for injury grievances, the final arbitrator in all disputes was Commissioner Pete Rozelle, hired and paid by the owners.

And then there were the minor indignities, like being locked up in a usually distant training camp for six weeks before the season. No other sport treated its supposedly adult athletes like that.

Young Ed Garvey, wise-cracking executive director of the Players' Association, spent the spring and early summer firing up his constituency. He had organized demonstrations as student body president at the University of Wisconsin some years earlier and he approached this crisis with the zeal and self-righteousness of a campus radical.

As the various NFL teams prepared to open training camp in July, their players went on strike.

Forewarned, the owners were prepared. Their drafted rookies, theoretically not yet members of the union, were persuaded to come to camp. Those who hesitated were threatened—illegally, as it turned out according to later rulings of the National Labor Relations Board—with the loss of their signing bonuses. Every team held open tryouts for free agents. Anyone who could walk received an audition, and some of these even managed to stick around when it was all over.

The union threatened to block the NFL's preseason schedule, a major source of revenue for the clubs, and they did force cancellation of the College All-Star game. But the rest of the exhibitions were played as usual, despite picket lines, with refunds to those fans who didn't want to see a lot of scrubeenies perform.

As the summer wore on, the strike crumbled. Some players, like the Colts' last rugged individual, Mike Curtis, opposed the union from the beginning. He had crossed picket lines three years earlier during the last strike. There were some who suspected, though, that if all the players voted to play, the stubborn redhead would have elected to strike by himself.

Whether for moral reasons or because they feared for their jobs under raw pressure from coaches, the players slowly trickled into camp. Eventually, the union would have to win its battles in court, which it did, and the long legal process finally ended with a new contract three years later.

Some militant players, most of them black, who perhaps felt the freedom issues more deeply and knew that a big paycheck did not always buy dignity, stayed out to the end. Most of the big-name quarterbacks came in early. Others, feeling the importance of rapport with their striking teammates, also remained out.

The Colts' quarterbacks, Domres and Jones, remained out together almost to the end. Until then the quarterbacking was handled by a couple of guys named Pierantozzi and Bobrowski.

During their holdout, Marty and Bert reportedly spoke often on the phone.

Neither, of course, wanted to allow the other the advantage of breaking ranks first, but it was obvious that the longer they stayed out, the better it was for Domres. Domres, the veteran, already knew how to play. It was Jones who needed the work, the three weeks of two-a-days that open every training camp, especially since he had missed this time with the All-Stars as a rookie the year before. Domres probably helped talk Jones into staying out longer than he might have otherwise for the best play-calling of the young veteran's career.

Domres had also done some pretty nifty off-field maneuvering during the spring.

A new entity had entered pro football that year, the World Football League, a shakily financed fast-buck enterprise created by the imaginative Gary Davidson. Davidson had previously formed the American Basketball Association and the World Hockey Association, both of which appeared to be more or less thriving. He would now bring his promotional gifts to football.

One look at blond, tanned Gary Davidson and you knew he had to be from southern California. Appearance meant more than substance to him. He was a lawyer with offices in Newport Beach, California, Nixon country, and the only surprise was that he had never joined that administration. He would have fit right in.

Davidson was an operator. He didn't give a damn about basketball, hockey, or football. When he organized a league, he always kept one franchise for himself, for free. As the league became operative, there was always one sucker so afraid of being left out that he would pay top dollar for Davidson's franchise. Total profit. Finders fees, legal fees, marketing fees—these also accrued to Davidson and his associates, who somehow always ended up out of the picture before long.

Unlike the American Football League, which had been soundly financed by men with a love for professional football, the WFL and its quick-buck guys largely ignored the college market. They took a page from the Al Davis blitz book to concentrate on signing big-name NFL players for future delivery, stars like Ken Stabler of the Oakland Raiders and Ted Hendricks of the Colts.

They also tried for others, like Marty Domres. The New York Stars, who didn't last the season in that city, made a big pitch for Marty. They reasoned he would be a big draw in New York because of his college rep. Also, he was approaching his option season and would be available for the WFL's second campaign.

Still not 100 percent certain that Jones would fulfill his potential, Joe Thomas could not afford to lose Domres. He pulled out his checkbook and matched zeros with the WFL to keep the young quarterback. Playing both sides adroitly, Domres eventually signed a long-term agreement with the Colts for a salary estimated at $100,000 annually. The WFL may have offered more, but Marty knew the Colts would be good for whatever they promised.

Domres had no qualms about using this unique situation to bludgeon the Colts into a super contract. A ball player has to make it when he can. When his resolve softened, he merely had to think back to an incident the previous summer.

The Colts were playing a preseason game in Atlanta and blew a 13-10 lead when the Falcons scored 24 points in the fourth quarter for a 34-20 victory. Two of those late Atlanta touchdowns came on interception returns against Domres, the second of which was particularly embarrassing since a defensive lineman, John Zook, picked it off and ran it in from the twenty.

The losing Colts were sitting glumly in their locker room when owner Bob Irsay came storming in and proceeded to give Domres a tongue-lashing in front of the entire team. The gist of the tirade was that Domres was masquerading as a pro football player. "You're lousy," the red-faced owner shouted at his player as the rest of the Colts writhed in shared embarrassment.

The incident, of course, became public. "He just sort of stopped me and gave me a personal critique. I was surprised. I never heard of anything like that happening in professional sports before," Domres said.

Domres at the time said he would let the incident "slide,"

but he warned, "This is just another experience making me a more hard-nosed football player." Less than a year later he got his chance to put the screws to the Colts. More ominous, the incident illustrated how Irsay could lose his temper and self-control when faced with defeat, even in preseason.

Hendricks was a different story. The Mad Stork, as he was known, went ahead and signed with the WFL and announced he was playing out his option with the Colts. Only Thomas changed the scenario a bit. Within weeks, Hendricks was playing out his option with Green Bay. Thomas traded him.

Thomas never had been enamored of Hendricks's freelance style of linebacking. He conceded the 6-foot-7 Stork, who used his height to bat down passes and block kicks, made some big plays. But he blew a lot of others and frequently made his teammates look bad by not always being where he was supposed to be. On top of this, Hendricks was a representative of the old regime.

In exchange for Hendricks, the Colts obtained another linebacker in Tom MacLeod, not spectacular but solid. All year long Thomas would tell people how well MacLeod was playing.

(Like Stabler, Hendricks and many of these future signees never played a down for the WFL. They took their up-front money, but as soon as their new connections missed a payment on the rest, they declared their contracts had been breached and they remained in the NFL. There is no public record of any of the up-front money ever being returned.)

Although the WFL didn't go after college players en masse, the new league, which died during its second season, was a visible presence on the sidelines. Agents of the collegians used the WFL alternative to get higher salaries for their clients.

NFL general managers and owners met privately with advisors for the top prospects to see what they would be demanding as they staged a secret preliminary draft.

Dallas, which owned Houston's lead-off choice from a previous trade, made no secret of its desire for Ed (Too Tall) Jones of Tennessee State, a can't-miss defensive lineman. San Diego was up next and needed help in the same area.

This was a good year for defensive linemen. John Dutton of Nebraska rated only fractions of a percentage point behind Jones in the computer printouts and Carl Barzilauskas of Indiana was just a shade behind him. Both Dutton and Barzilauskas were handled by an aggressive agent, Howard Slusher. The Chargers were really interested in Dutton, but learned before the formal draft that Slusher would be seeking a contract worth more than $300,000 for his boy. Barzilauskas would be in the same high-priced neighborhood.

The Chargers, struggling financially, decided to look elsewhere. They opted for Bo Matthews, a fullback from Clemson who has never fulfilled that kind of first-round promise. Drafting third, the Giants went for John Hicks, a guard from Ohio State. The Bears followed with Waymond Bryant, a well-regarded linebacker who had played with Too Tall Jones at Tennessee State.

The Colts were up next and Joe Thomas quickly pounced on Dutton, a 6-foot-7, 266-pound giant with a deceptive baby face who was able to psych himself up for great deeds of violence on the football field.

Dutton's father, an engineer, played football in college, did some boxing, and lifted weights well into middle age. His son early on got interested in sports in Rapid City, South Dakota, and his first game was basketball. But as John became more muscular and more ferocious, he realized his skills were more outstanding in football. "I could jump and

I could shoot in basketball, but so could a lot of people and I knew there were kids from the big cities who could probably do it better," he pointed out. He also discovered a hot temper that surfaced during competition and decided, "I'll probably be better off in football."

Out of some eighty offers, he chose to attend Nebraska, a national powerhouse. Dutton is an outdoor person, but he rarely joins the Bert Jones hunting parties. "I prefer to spend my days off with my wife," he says and they make an eye-catching couple. Ginny Dutton, training to be a ballet dancer, is barely five feet tall.

The Colts also owned the Rams' first-round choice in the 1974 draft and Joe Thomas took a flyer on a flyer with that selection. He had scouted the East–West Shrine game in San Francisco and he remembered a swift jug-eared receiver from Louisiana Tech running away from all the defensive backs. "The fastest white guy we've ever seen," they said in awe.

Impressed with Carr's speed, Thomas picked him after Dutton. He smiled to himself when people asked, "Who the hell is Roger Carr?" They soon would know.

The story of Roger Carr is fascinating and inspirational.

"My parents were divorced when I was a year old and I never knew my real father until I was sixteen," Roger relates. "My mother remarried and my stepfather was a tool-pusher on an oil rig. He was a good provider, but he was never home. My mother worked as a hairdresser and she was seldom home, either, so I was always on my own. I could come and go as I pleased. People think kids like that, but they don't. They want discipline. They want someone to show that they care.

"From the time I was old enough to walk I was in all sports. I could always run, throw, do anything I wanted, but what I needed was a father. My father was never there to take me to my games like the other fathers."

Roger's crisis began when he was finishing his sophomore year in high school in Enid, Oklahoma. He had been all-state in basketball, excelled in football and baseball in the top level of Oklahoma schoolboy competition, and he had just won the state decathlon championship in track.

"People thought I had everything," he says, but, in fact, his life was empty. The highlight of his existence was a brief annual visit from his father's parents. "They would only stay for a few hours, but I could tell they were interested in me. I felt they loved me more than anyone."

That summer, he asked his grandparents if he could come and live with them in the tiny hamlet of Cotton Valley, Louisiana, which happened to be only thirty miles from Ruston. They agreed.

Although they were in their sixties, Roger's grandparents gave him the first real discipline he had ever known. And strength. He would need all of it.

That's because word soon got out to neighboring towns that Cotton Valley had just imported this hotshot athlete from a big school in Oklahoma. People in northern Louisiana take their high school sports seriously. They didn't want to risk losing to this ringer. Although Carr's grandparents had assumed legal guardianship of the boy, he was ruled ineligible for scholastic competition for a full year as a transfer student because he was not living with his natural parents.

To a fifteen-year-old whose entire life had been athletics, the decision was devastating. They made him the team manager, but this was almost worse than nothing. He grew to hate his new friends for being able to compete. "For the first time in my life my ability had been taken away from me and I had nothing to fall back on," he says. His grades plummeted. He started drinking, fighting, skipping school. He became known as the village troublemaker. "The only thing I missed was drugs and I figure that was only because they hadn't gotten to Cotton Valley yet," he says.

However, Carr's grandparents were devout churchgoers and they insisted that Roger attend Sunday services regularly for the first time in his life. "I sure didn't want to go, but they had this great ol' preacher there in the First Baptist church and as I sat there in the back row I began to realize that my life wasn't going anywhere. Then, about three-fourths of the way through my junior year, one Sunday morning I felt he was preaching just to me. He said the Lord had a purpose for us, all of us. Well, I knew He'd given me athletic talent, that this was my gift. I had always been No. 1 and now He had taken everything away from me. The Lord had humbled me so much, maybe to make me realize what I had."

The experience in that little Baptist church produced a transformation in Roger Carr. His failing grades turned to As and Bs, but too late to salvage his high school football career. Because of all his failures, he lacked half a point of being scholastically eligible to compete in his senior season. However, with the new semester, he was able to play the last five games of the basketball schedule, averaging thirty points a game.

Cotton Valley did not have a track team, but one spring afternoon while studying in the library, Roger overheard one of the coaches asking the principal for time off to attend the district meet.

"This is where the Lord comes in because it took a miracle," Roger says. "A voice said to me, 'You've got to go to that meet.'"

Although he had not practiced his specialty, the long

jump, for two years, Roger pleaded for a chance to compete. He knew how many hours of practice are required just to get down the intricate footwork for this event, but he had to go. The coach consented and Roger won with a perfect jump.

This qualified Carr for the regionals, where he won again to move on to the state meet. And there he won again with a record leap. The coach of Louisiana Tech was watching and he offered Roger a track scholarship, which was accepted.

Then, one day at Louisiana Tech, Carr asked the football coach if he could do some punting for the team. He made the squad and soon afterwards the whole group was called on to run wind sprints. Roger Carr was the fastest man on the team. They threw him some footballs and he caught them. Roger Carr became a wide receiver and some summer days in the off-season he worked out with a young pro quarterback who lived in town, Bert Jones.

The Colts also owned two draft choices in the second round, and with the first of these Thomas pulled another surprise. He had taken defensive linemen with two of his first three picks in 1973 and another with his lead-off choice in '74.

Now he grabbed another, Fred Cook, a defensive end from Southern Mississippi. Cook weighed only 235 and ran the forty in an impressive 4.8 seconds. Most scouts projected him as a linebacker and rated him lower in the draft because of the expected position change. But Thomas figured Cook could bulk up another ten pounds and play on the line. He was right. At 246, Cook became a regular on the Colts' front four. He and Dutton became the starting ends as rookies. Barnes moved from end to tackle next to Joe Ehrmann.

Thomas had his quarterback in Bert Jones and his front four. The foundation was complete.

The rest of the Colts' 1974 draft also was productive. On the third round, Thomas chose Robert Pratt, a guard from North Carolina, who eventually became a regular, and further down there were three players who would serve as subs on the play-off teams—guard Bob Van Dyne, linebacker Dan Dickel, and receiver Freddie Scott. There also was some public interest in Baltimore's seventeenth and last selection, a wide receiver named Tim Berra. Berra, who lasted one season, was the son of baseball Hall of Famer, Yogi Berra.

Another newcomer was Toni Linhart, a blond Austrian who had given up a successful career as a professional soccer player in Europe to seek his fortune in America as a place-kicker. Linhart, an architect, had almost made the 1960 Austrian Olympic ski team, so he was a pretty good athlete. But he flunked his first NFL trial with the Saints in 1972. No wonder. "I didn't know a thing about American football then," he says. "Wide receivers and free safeties were a mystery to me. I couldn't even speak the language. All I knew how to do was kick the ball." But he kept trying and four years later he was kicking in the Pro Bowl.

Even without the exacerbation of the strike, the scene in Baltimore was hardly tranquil as the season opener approached. There was still brisk competition at quarterback between Jones and Domres. In fact, there was competition and bickering up and down the line and some of the old Colts were still missing their friends and actively resenting the newcomers. "I don't think anybody got along too well those days," Stan White recalls.

The problems extended beyond the players. Thomas was not that enchanted with Schnellenberger, his choice, but his third choice, as head coach. Schnellenberger, a rigid, colorless drillmaster, had tried to install the Miami system in toto in Baltimore without anything even resembling Miami personnel. Schnellenberger was so into football that on game weekends away from home he seldom even knew the name of the hotel where the team was staying. Or cared. All he needed was an electric outlet in his room so he could plug in his projector and study film.

All through 1973, Thomas had pressured Schnellenberger to give the young players more time. Then, in the off-season, Thomas demanded that Schnellenberger fire all of his defensive assistants. Schnellenberger, loyal and a man of integrity, at first resisted. But then Thomas told him, in effect, it's them or you. And Howard knew that if he was fired, the entire staff would be let go anyway. At least he could save the jobs of half of them.

When the 1974 campaign opened, the battle to get young players into the lineup continued. In camp, Roger Carr had pulled a hamstring muscle in his leg. Schnellenberger thought the rookie was taking too long to recover. They had words. Carr would have been cut if Thomas had not interceded. Then, for the opener, Schnellenberger named Domres as his starting quarterback.

The 1974 season began poorly. Domres suffered bruised ribs in the first quarter and Jones replaced him but neither was able to put a point on the scoreboard in a 30-0 loss to the Steelers in Pittsburgh. A week later, in the home opener, Domres started again and was trailing 20-6 when Jones entered the game in the fourth quarter. Bert completed one touchdown pass to Bill Olds but then threw an end zone interception that killed Baltimore's last chance to avoid a 20-13 defeat.

After the game, the coaches were critical of Domres but said he would continue to start. Jones, openly unhappy, was quoted as saying he still considered himself the "No. 1 quarterback."

The following Sunday, the Colts moved on to Philadelphia and again Domres was the starting quarterback. The Eagles are noted for their official hospitality and for the first half Irsay shared a private box on the press level with Joe Thomas. In most games, Irsay usually stayed put for the first two quarters and then meandered down to the sidelines to be closer to the action for the second half.

At half time, the Colts trailed, 13-3, and Domres had not played well. Irsay and Thomas were not alone in speculating that Schnellenberger would have to switch to Jones for the second half.

They were wrong. Schnellenberger stuck with Domres to open the third period. However, what they and almost everyone in the stadium did not know was that Schnellenberger had told Jones he was going into the game if Domres did not score on the Colts' first possession. Jones, in fact, was warming up behind the bench.

By this time, however, Irsay was on the sidelines and as the Colts moved to the attack behind Domres, he approached his coach.

"When are you going to play Bert?" he asked innocently enough.

The question shattered Schnellenberger's concentration and poise. All the emotion and upset he had been absorbing all these months exploded out of control.

"Get out of here!" he screamed at his embarrassed owner. "Who the hell do you think you are? Get the hell out of here! Go back upstairs where you belong."

And with this he made a sweeping gesture like a baseball umpire ejecting a player from the field, fist clenched, thumb up.

"Oh, my God, you should see what Schnellenberger just did to Irsay," a Colts scout in the press box exclaimed.

Schnellenberger had just thrown his owner out of the game.

Worse, he had done it openly and obviously in front of more than 66,000 people. Most didn't notice, of course, but Bob Irsay, the millionaire, knew they were there.

Irsay had paid $19 million to stand on the sidelines, but he didn't really belong there. Few owners or general managers ever ventured into this special area of the coach's turf, especially during the heat of the game, strictly to avoid this sort of thing.

Shocked by Schnellenberger's outburst, Irsay backed off and returned to the press box.

He fumed as Domres remained in the game. He may have thought Schnellenberger was deliberately defying him, but really the coach had no choice. Everyone on the bench had heard the owner's question and Howard's profane retort. Now he could not make a quarterback change even if he wished. It would be interpreted as an open surrender of his authority to run the team. He would be finished as an effective coach.

Domres completed the third period and Joe Lavender returned an intercepted pass thirty-seven yards for the decisive touchdown. Bert finally got in for the fourth quarter and completed a meaningless touchdown pass to Glenn Doughty in the 30-10 loss.

Irsay was furious as the second half progressed. He had been publicly humiliated. He talked to Thomas of firing Schnellenberger on the spot and related the sideline conversation. "No man can tell an owner this and get away with it," he grumbled.

Thomas, for his part, argued against such a move. It would accomplish nothing and probably wreck the rest of the season. He knew Irsay had been off base by interfering on the sidelines and he felt he could eventually control Schnellenberger and force him to play the young kids. He spoke soothingly to Irsay and thought he had talked him out of a rash move.

As the game ended, Irsay bolted from the owner's box and caught the first elevator down to the locker room level. Thomas took his time. He thought he had averted any crisis.

The players trooped glumly into the spacious locker room in Philadelphia's Veterans Stadium and waited for Schnellenberger's postgame comments. They were brief.

"The offense stunk, the defense stunk, the special teams stunk. I'll see ya Monday," said the coach of the 0-and-3 Colts as he turned to his own room to shower and dress.

Now the players were stripping away their tape and sweaty uniforms. It was quiet. Reporters still had not been admitted.

Suddenly the dressing room door flew open.

It was Irsay, red-faced and fuming. His team had been humiliated, therefore he had been humiliated. And his coach had cursed him out.

According to one observer, Irsay's tirade went something like this:

"I have never seen such bull in my life. Dammit, you guys couldn't beat a high school team. I feel like suiting up and playing myself. I'm sick and tired of all this and as of now I'm firing Howard Schnellenberger. Joe Thomas is going to be your new head coach, effective immediately."

The players took Irsay's opening remarks in silence. They knew they had been playing badly and probably deserved to be chewed out. But their mood changed when they realized Irsay was making a coaching change. They liked Schnellenberger. They realized a mid-season change meant writing off the rest of the year. "No, no, no!" they exclaimed.

This defiance made Irsay even more angry.

"If you guys don't like it, I'll trade you all, I'll put you on waivers for a dollar, I don't give a damn," he screamed. "Just give me a call tomorrow if you don't like it, just give me a call."

In the coaches' room with Schnellenberger, Ernie Accorsi, then the Colts' public relations director, heard the turmoil. At first he thought a couple of the players had gotten into a fight. Then he heard clearly the final words of Irsay's opening statement, "Thomas is going to be your new head coach effective immediately."

"What the hell's going on out there?" asked Schnellenberger, who had been given a vote of confidence as coach by Thomas just eleven days earlier.

"I'm not sure," Accorsi replied, "but I think you've just been fired."

The players had learned of the change before Schnellenberger, which is not exactly protocol, but Irsay soon took care of that oversight. He marched into the back room. "I'm firing you, Howard, and naming Joe Thomas head coach, effective right now," Irsay declaimed and spun on his heel and walked out.

As he left the dressing room, Irsay blundered into the clutch of sports writers, angry because they had been kept outside longer than the period specified by league rules. Irsay repeated his announcement for them: "I have just fired the coach. There was no other way. The Baltimore Colts will go on that field to win even if I have to play myself." Then he stormed away.

Later in the week, Irsay explained to Cameron Snyder, colorful football writer of the Baltimore Sun, "There was no reason for him to use that kind of language. All I asked this man was 'Do you think you'll play Bert Jones?' He jumped all over me like a cat. . . . I won't tolerate such language from anyone [and] I don't think you would, either. Some people say I was drunk. That simply is not true. I had a drink but I was sober as hell."

When the writers finally poured into the dressing room, Thomas still had not appeared. He was taking a leisurely trip down, certain the crisis had been averted.

"You can't believe what I had to stop today," he told Accorsi when he finally appeared.

"You didn't stop it," his young PR aide replied drily. "You're the new head coach."

Finally, about half an hour later, the dressing room was cleared. The players were reclaiming their valuables from the equipment manager. Schnellenberger, red-eyed and tie-less, his shirt half buttoned, had long since departed without a word. The team physician was driving him back to Baltimore. Howard had more than 1½ years left on his contract and he would be paid.

Thomas now climbed on a trunk to address his new team.

He said the day's events had not been instigated by him, that he had been taken by surprise as much as anyone but that "we're going to get this thing on the right track."

"Well, if you had nothing to do with all this, why don't you reverse it?" outspoken Mike Curtis challenged from the floor.

Thomas said this could not be done.

"Well, what the hell are you going to do?" Curtis continued sarcastically. "What do you think all this is going to do to our young players?"

Thomas has a short fuse, too. "Look," he snapped, "there's nothing we can do about this. I'm the head coach—and that's the way it's going to be."

But he would remember Mike Curtis.

The players continued to mumble profanely as they finished packing. Roger Carr, the rookie from Cotton Valley, had thought he was really getting into the big time when he turned pro. Now he wondered. Stan White felt the same way. "This is professional football?" he asked himself. Glenn Doughty noted that he had been a professional three seasons and this was his fourth head coach. He tried to count up all the assistants who had passed through, and gave up.

The Colts had made this short road trip by bus. As they rode home, they gathered in little groups to talk quietly. They knew they were doomed to another losing season. Their motivation would have to come from within. They would have to work at perfecting their own skills.

Both quarterbacks, when asked, spoke up in Schnellenberger's defense. They said they thought he should have been retained.

As soon as he took over his unexpected new duties, Thomas made one move that eased some of the players' hostility. On the trip back to Baltimore he queried the various assistants for suggestions. They agreed on one thing. Schnellenberger had been working the players too hard. His practice sessions dragged on interminably. Players who are tired and bored do not learn.

At his first team meeting in Baltimore, Thomas announced that henceforth workouts would last no longer than ninety minutes.

Thomas also disclosed that his assistants would do most of the on-field coaching—and that Bert Jones would start at quarterback the following week against New England and would continue to call most of his own plays.

Thomas also decided that since he was wearing a second hat as head coach, he would really wear a hat as head coach. He had the equipment man dig out a blue Colts' baseball cap for him to wear at practice. It didn't fit quite right, but Joe Thomas wore it anyway. "It was too big and it sat down on his ears and you couldn't see his eyes under the brim," one player remembers.

There was a lot about the job that didn't fit.

For one thing, Thomas didn't really know the terminology for the plays. "Tell him to call that end run—[or]—that little screen pass," he would instruct a player going into the game. The messenger would be smirking when he got to the huddle.

Thomas also continued to approach his job as a personnel man. In pregame talks, he would discuss the opposition this way: "Well, their right guard can't be much, he was only a sixth-round draft choice—and their left guard, heck, they signed him as a free agent." Aware that the left guard had developed into an all-pro, the players could only sit and wonder.

Once the game began, Thomas proved highly excitable on the sidelines, which doesn't exactly set him apart from many of his more experienced and distinguished colleagues. Once a long touchdown pass from Jones to Carr was nullified by a holding penalty. Thomas ran out on the field, picked up the official's flag, and threw it at him. That drew another handkerchief for unsportsmanlike conduct. Thomas repeated his act and drew another fifteen-yard levy. "We ended up something like fourth-and-sixty," a player recalls.

Players say Thomas quickly jerked players from the lineup for a single mistake, a tactic not calculated to breed confidence, but the real trouble was that since he wasn't involved in the day-to-day coaching he often blamed the wrong man for a breakdown. "Three-quarters of the time he'd be yelling at the wrong guy," players charged.

Still, the players respected Thomas for the way he plunged

into an assignment he had neither sought nor was suited for. "He's got guts," they agreed.

The Colts were blown out of their first game under Thomas by New England, 42-3, but they were competitive the rest of the way. They beat the Jets after five straight losses (two under Thomas) and later bested Atlanta, 17-7, behind Marty Domres as Thomas strutted up and down the sidelines during the closing minutes chortling, "The hay is in the barn; the hay is in the barn."

Domres was playing this particular game because Jones had suffered a dislocated right shoulder against Cincinnati two weeks earlier. But Bert returned for the last three weeks of the season. He was shut out by the Bills, 6-0, and then lost a 17-16 heartbreaker to the Dolphins.

The season ended against the Jets in Baltimore on December 15.

Before the kickoff, Thomas called Jones aside and told him to disregard the game plan.

"Forget about everything. I just want you to go out there and throw the ball all over the field," Thomas ordered his young quarterback.

Bert took him at his word. He had been given a new toy and he came out gunning. This was his game. Although he was intercepted three times in the first half, Bert ended up completing thirty-six passes in fifty-three attempts, both club records, for 385 yards. He passed for four touchdowns and ran for a fifth. Along the way he set an NFL record with seventeen straight completions as Lydell Mitchell broke Raymond Berry's club record with thirteen catches. Lydell's big day also enabled him to win the NFL title with seventy-two receptions for the year, a league record for running backs.

Meanwhile, Joe Namath was also having himself a day for

the Jets, completing nineteen of twenty-eight for 281 yards and two touchdowns. The two teams ended up with 840 yards in combined total offense.

Even though the Jets won, 45-38, to send Baltimore home with a 2-12 record, it had been fun football, especially for Bert.

"It was the kind of game that made you want to come back the next season, the kind to make you want to not stop playing," he declared.

Exactly what Joe Thomas had had in mind.

9
Looney Tunes

—

Bert Jones wasn't the only Baltimore Colt who felt the 1974 season had ended too soon. Joe Thomas, nervous, hyperactive, survivor of open heart surgery only a few years before, a man who spoke in short bursts with hands fluttering and eyes darting, decided he would like to stay on as coach.

His friends were flabbergasted. Does a man with TB volunteer to work in a coal mine? After Thomas's gritty performance as interim coach the past season, he had won over many of the once-hostile Baltimore fans. Why risk losing them again? Why risk his health?

Thomas, however, was convinced he had done a great job as coach despite his 2-9 record and, indeed, he had in one respect by keeping the Colts competitive. On a postseason visit to Chicago to discuss the coaching situation with Bob Irsay, Thomas volunteered to stay on in the dual capacity.

However, for doing this, Thomas felt that his salary, already over $100,000 a year, should be increased by one-half. He wanted a $50,000 raise, which is about what they would have had to pay a new coach anyway.

This request gave Irsay the excuse he needed to tell his GM to go back to the front office and hire someone else to handle the troops in the field.

Getting a coach did not take long. On January 15, one month to the day after the Colts' last game, forty-four-year-old Ted Marchibroda was named head coach with a three-year contract. "It didn't matter which way I analyzed the situation, Ted Marchibroda's name kept surfacing as the top choice," Thomas told the press.

Marchibroda, low-keyed as a coach and a devoted family man, had impeccable credentials beyond the historic-trivia fact that he had once beaten out John Unitas for a quarterback job.

He had grown up in football country just outside Pittsburgh and played his first two years of varsity football at St. Bonaventure. When the Bonnies dropped football, he transferred to the University of Detroit for his final season of eligibility, but then he returned to his original school to graduate.

As one of the nation's leading passers at Detroit, he was a first-round draft choice of the Steelers in 1953, but an arm injury brought an end to his career after he spent 1957 with the Chicago Cardinals.

Marchibroda turned to coaching in 1961 as backfield coach under Bill McPeak in Washington and spent four years there before joining the staff of George Allen in Los Angeles. In 1971 he moved east with Allen to Washington as offensive coordinator. Fourteen years as an NFL assistant, ten of them under the demanding George Allen. Marchibroda had paid his dues.

Along the line he had worked with such outstanding quarterbacks as Roman Gabriel, Sonny Jurgensen, and Billy Kilmer. He knew quarterbacks and he knew how to put an offense together. This was not lost on Thomas or Bert Jones. To run his defense, Marchibroda brought along a sharp young associate from Washington, balding Maxie Baughan.

Because the oldest of his four children were still in high

school and he didn't want to disrupt their schooling at this sensitive point, Marchibroda let his family remain in nearby Washington for the time being, a period that stretched out over two years. He moved to Baltimore alone, going home on weekends in the off-season, and this gave him time to throw himself whole-heartedly into his job.

Ted's first task was to survey films of the Colts in action over the last couple of years and this study made it evident that Bert Jones was a quarterback of limitless future. His second action was to summon Bert to Baltimore for several days in February. He did not want to wait until July to start to tap that future.

Their first meeting was devoted to orientation, a get-acquainted sort of deal, but later that spring for five weeks in April and May, Bert returned for a concentrated course on how to play quarterback.

They did not get into mechanics at all.

"All quarterbacks have their own style," Marchibroda explains. "When you get to this stage, they all know how to take the snap from center and hand off and Bert certainly had the ability to throw the football and to run with it.

"The thing is, as I like to say, you can play quarterback before you can *play* quarterback. You can line up under the center and take the ball and say you're playing quarterback, or you can play quarterback from the aspect that everything you're doing is [involved] in the ball game. It's a thinking game and this is where we had to work with Bert, on the thinking aspect of it."

Marchibroda claims he never doubted that Bert would be a receptive student, but one wonders. Bert by now had played two seasons in the NFL. He had played the game on an organized basis for ten years and had lived intimately with pro football for years before that. Many people thought he was pretty good already, that it was just a shame he was surrounded by such an incompetent cast. They told him so, too. Bert could have been as tough to coach as he supposedly was during his early years at LSU.

On the other hand, Marchibroda knew he had some pretty impressive credits of his own to lay before the young quarterback. He had been a quarterback, too, and a pretty good one who had made the most of unspectacular physical gifts. And he had worked with all those good quarterbacks. Marchibroda also made it a point to remind Jones that "I had been in Los Angeles where Roman Gabriel was the quarterback for four years and he hadn't had a lot of success until we got there." Bert knew full well that he was coming off a 2-12 season and that the Colts' overall record since he joined them was 6-22. Only one of those victories had come over a team with a winning record.

That established, Marchibroda also had to make certain Jones realized his new coach had a great deal of respect for him as an individual talent and as a quarterback prospect in his own right. From the very beginning, Marchibroda told him, "Bert, I don't want you to be like Roman Gabriel or Sonny Jurgensen or Billy Kilmer. I want you to be yourself and play your game."

Marchibroda thinks that this was very important to Bert. "I think this is what he wanted to hear," Ted says. "He wanted the responsibility of the ball club and he was very hopeful that I would give it to him. He is a very responsible kid and he was then, too, at age twenty-three."

The daily sessions followed a pattern over the next five weeks. Each day would be devoted to a different phase of the offense: the strong-side passing attack, the weak-side passing attack, the short yardage game, the two-minute game—all the technical gibberish that announcers on television like to spout. But meaningful. During these lessons, as an adjunct Bert also was picking up a pretty good idea of how various NFL teams played defense, and why, and how to attack them.

Bert would show up around nine in the morning. He and Ted would look at films illustrating the day's topic for an hour or so and then attack the blackboard. They closed with an open discussion of what they had seen. During these talks, game situations might come up. Why, faced with the same down and distance and defense, would Gabriel do one thing here and another thing there? By noon at the latest they quit for the day. That was it.

Marchibroda knew full well any quarterback could learn a series of plays and checkoffs any given week as part of his game plan and if he was too dumb even for that, the coaches could call everything from the bench. But he wanted more from Bert.

"I wanted him to know our system and mostly *why* we are doing what we are doing," Ted explained. "When the season rolled around I assumed he would know when to apply what we had been talking about. It was like going to school for five weeks."

As the sessions dragged on, Marchibroda marveled at Bert's enthusiasm and concentration.

"That's the thing that impressed me most about this period," he would say later. "At that time of year, a man can very easily become bored with football. Bert never did. He was very intense and very willing to learn whatever we had to teach him.

"Bert is the type of individual that whatever he does he does with the so-called 110 percent that we talk about. The reason for his success in football season is that he works hard at his profession. He looks at a lot of film and gives it 110 percent in all aspects. During the season he comes in at nine-thirty in the morning and leaves at five, five-thirty in the evening. After he goes hunting on Tuesday, he always comes by the office that night to pick up the new film to study at home. He never misses a Tuesday.

"Once the season is over, he is quite capable of forgetting football and getting into those other fields he's interested in and then he gives that his 110 percent. But during our meetings that spring he devoted himself to learning football."

When Bert returned to Louisiana, Ted Marchibroda knew that Bert's mental approach to the game would equal his physical skills. He told his assistant coaches, "We've got a pretty good quarterback on our hands."

Ted's next task was to modify the system he had brought from Washington to fit Bert's particular talents and those of his teammates, but he continued to stress the mental side of the game.

When the Colts gathered in training camp, Marchibroda told reporters, "If we're going to be successful, I'm going to have to make Bert Jones thirty years of age before the season is over."

On a foggy December day in Baltimore five months later, Marchibroda and the world would see that transformation. But we're getting ahead of ourselves.

Those seminars were a revelation to Jones. He had grown up with pro football but this was the first time someone had sat down with him to explain why certain things worked. And once you knew why, then you could build an offense to make things happen instead of just reacting like an automaton to whatever keys the defense wanted to show you.

"It's like calculus," Bert explained. "Someone has to show you how to do it, but once you know, it's easy."

Now that he had found a coach, Joe Thomas went back

to finding players. There was a draft to get ready for and the Colts would be choosing first, thanks to a coin flip with the Giants and their 2-12 record.

From the start there was pressure on Thomas to use that lead-off pick to select Randy White, an outstanding prospect from the nearby University of Maryland. Scouts projected White as either a defensive end or a linebacker with a "can't-miss" label in either spot. In most college defensive alignments, the ends have a lot of what the pros would consider linebacking responsibility. That's why so many small college ends become successful pro linebackers. In the case of Fred Cook, who could have been a linebacker, the Colts had built him up and he remained a swift down lineman.

Thomas, though, felt the Colts were well stocked at both positions White could fill and what he needed was help in the offensive line to keep Bert Jones in one piece.

Another master plan hatched in his fertile mind.

The class quarterback in the college draft was Steve Bartkowski, a late bloomer from the University of California. The Falcons, who were drafting third, were desperate for a quarterback. Joe's philosophy is that you never overlook a top quarterback if he's available in the draft, just as baseball teams maintain you can never have enough pitching. Maybe he was bluffing, but he made certain that Atlanta, one of the NFL's perennial joke franchises, got his message loud and clear. If they wanted to be sure of a shot at Bartkowski they had better talk to Joe Thomas. They talked.

On the eve of the college draft, the Falcons traded their all-pro offensive tackle, George Kunz, and their own first-round draft choice to Baltimore for the Colts' number one. They got their quarterback, Bartkowski, and the Colts got a solid and experienced tackle while dropping down only two places in the drafting line. Picking second with a choice they had obtained from the Giants, the Cowboys took Randy White, which relieved Thomas of the pressure to take the local boy as his opening selection.

With the third choice in the whole draft, the Colts selected another offensive lineman to help Jones, highly regarded Ken Huff of North Carolina.

Kunz became an outstanding addition to the Colts, not only as a player of all-pro ability, but as a stabilizing influence on all the young talent Thomas had collected.

At first, Kunz wasn't too happy about the trade.

"Why Baltimore?" he asked himself plaintively when Falcon coach Marion Campbell called to inform him of the deal. George knew Atlanta was one of the weakest teams in the NFL and that Baltimore was one of only two that were worse.

There was another shock when he got to the Colts' training camp. With the Falcons he had been considered one of the team's younger players. In Baltimore, his seven years made him one of the oldest guys on the squad, in the top five, in fact.

But he quickly established rapport with Marchibroda's new line coach, Whitey Dovall, and slowly the realization came to him that this young Baltimore eleven was ready for better things.

Kunz is a picture athlete, 6 foot 6, 260 pounds, blond, handsome, and muscular, but he came late to athletics.

George's father was killed in an accident when he was two months old and his mother went to live with her parents in Los Angeles. George's grandfather died when he was nine and so, essentially, the two women brought him up. He grew very close to his mother and at fourteen chose to enter a seminary to become a priest. To that point the major male influences in George's life had come through his parochial school Boy Scout troop.

After two years, though, George's mother was ill, and on weekends home from the seminary to visit her he would spend time socially with his old school friends. The football games they attended on Friday nights made an impression. "I felt I was missing something and if I felt that way I thought maybe I should be someplace else," George says in explaining his decision to leave the seminary.

He then enrolled at Loyola High School in Los Angeles for his junior year. The adjustment was not easy, but it could have been more difficult if George, on his first day in school, had not been introduced to the football coach. The sixteen-year-old former seminarian stood 6 foot 4 and weighed 215 pounds. "The coach asked me quickly if I wanted to try out for the team," Kunz recalls with a smile.

The next week he tried out. The coach asked which boys wanted to play offensive end. This seemed like a good spot so George raised his hand. The coach looked at him. "You're a tackle." "I've been a tackle ever since," Kunz says with the offensive lineman's passive shrug.

George indicates he was a nervous, aggressive kid when he came out of the seminary. Football provided him with an outlet and eased the transition. After workouts he was too tired to do anything but study and flop into bed. He did well on the gridiron and that gave him instant status among his new schoolmates. His first season, Loyola went undefeated and George made all-conference. As a senior, he lost only once and made all-state. Several schools recruited Kunz, but Notre Dame was the only Catholic institution among them so that's where he went.

Kunz was an outstanding student-athlete at Notre Dame. He was a dean's list, cum laude graduate in communications and philosophy, an academic all-America, team captain, and two-time consensus all-America. When he finished college he was the second player chosen in the 1969 draft behind O. J. Simpson.

Today he still remembers and recognizes "the men who were not my father who helped to guide me."

This was not a vintage draft for Thomas. After two years Huff still was not a regular, but the Colts did get a steal down in the fifth round.

Roosevelt Leaks had been one of the most outstanding fullbacks in University of Texas history and made all-America and finished third in the Heisman Trophy voting as a junior. But that spring he tore up his knee and he barely made it back for spot duty as a senior after surgery. Until the injury he was a sure first-round choice but now most pro teams shied away from him because of the operation. When he saw Leaks's name still there for the fifth round among a pretty slim crop of collegians, Thomas decided to take a chance. Although he would never be the player he might have been before he was hurt, by his second season Leaks was starting for the Colts as a workmanlike fullback.

Thomas went the trade and waiver route for additional reinforcements.

Ed George had been a fourth-round draft choice by the Steelers out of Wake Forest in 1970 but had elected instead to go to Canada, where he built quite a reputation as an offensive lineman. Now he wanted to return to the United States, and in April the Colts got his rights from Pittsburgh for a couple of future draft choices. George filled in well for several games in '75 before being sent on his way.

Then, in July, Thomas achieved what turned out to be a major coup when he obtained linebacker Jim Cheyunski from Buffalo for a sixth-round pick. Cheyunski was not very big and he had a history of knee problems and the Bills thought they had drafted some nifty young prospects to replace him. They virtually gave Cheyunski away, but Jim soon became a key member of the Colts' defense at middle linebacker and a major inspirational factor the way he performed week after week despite agonizing pain from his bad knees.

The week before the season opener, there was another flurry of activity in camp. Thomas dealt for 5-foot-5 kick returner Howard Stevens from New Orleans and for center Forrest Blue from San Francisco, both for draft choices. Blue was supposed to beat out incumbent Ken Mendenhall with no difficulty but he couldn't do it even though Thomas pushed Marchibroda hard on the matter.

The Colts also picked up two defensive backs off the waiver wire, and both became almost instant regulars in what was the weakest area of Baltimore's squad. Lloyd Mumphord was claimed from Miami, where he had been the Dolphins' fifth back, and took over at left corner. Jackie Wallace, imported from Minnesota for the same $100 fee, had never been able to crack the Vikings' secondary as a cornerback despite several opportunities when regulars were injured. The Colts moved him to free safety, a less demanding spot, and his performance improved.

With all these changes, including a new coach and staff, the Colts were feeling their way in training camp and during the preseason. They went into overtime to beat Denver in their first exhibition game, but then they lost three in a row, the last a one-sided 27-3 defeat by the Saints in New Orleans.

This was a humiliating setback for Bert Jones, playing back before the home folks. He obtained dozens of tickets for relatives and friends and failed even to produce a touchdown. He departed the game with his shirt half ripped off and his spirits dragging as well.

A Baltimore paper that week asked in an eight-column headline: "Will Bert Jones Deliver Promise?" The subhead noted: "Colt Fans Seek Production—Now."

Even though they didn't go to the preseason games when they had the chance, as Carroll Rosenbloom could bitterly testify, Colt fans and some of the newspapers took these games seriously. So, too, as it developed, did Bob Irsay.

Marchibroda, however, remained patient. He conceded Bert had played poorly against the Saints—maybe he was pressing too hard before the home fans—but he would not blame him for the two previous losses during which the Colts had been putting in only part of their offense. Marchibroda said he would continue to let Bert call his own plays.

The next week the Colts beat Houston, a brawling, physical gang, the day after Bert's twenty-fourth birthday, and Marchibroda felt more confident about the character of the team he had taken over.

The Colts then lost their exhibition windup to Washington, but snapped back to win the regular-season opener by routing the Bears in Chicago, 35-7. Bert was superb, completing fifteen of twenty-four passes for 177 yards and two touchdowns. Older observers recalled that Bert's daddy once had enjoyed a pretty good afternoon himself against the Bears.

On his way into the locker room, Bert gave a sports writer a friendly jab in the shoulder. "What do you think of that?" he asked. "Thirty-five points! Looks good, doesn't it?" The quarterback's spirits were revived.

They didn't stay revived very long, however. Although Bert continued to play fairly well, the Colts started losing. They dropped close games to two tough opponents, Oakland and Los Angeles, and then lost twice in a row to teams in their own division, Buffalo and New England. These defeats really hurt.

The losing streak by now had reached four and Ted Marchibroda was worried. He knew losing feeds on itself. "When you're losing, you stay down; but winners come out of it," he says. Marchibroda often talks in aphorisms, like his old mentor, George Allen, and, like Allen, likes to throw in baseball corollaries. The Colts were at the crossroads going up to New York to play the Jets.

Here, against a team that had won its last six games the previous season, the Colts showed what they were capable of. The offense, shackled the week before, gained 400 yards and the defense sacked Joe Namath seven times, the most in Joe's career, in a 45-28 victory.

The following week the Colts beat Cleveland in Baltimore as Bert threw a couple of touchdown passes for two in a row.

They got quite a shock the next Sunday up in Buffalo, however. Less than two minutes into the second period they found themselves trailing the Bills, 21-0, on three touchdowns by O. J. Simpson. Two of the scores came on passes from Joe Ferguson to The Juice in a span of fifty-five seconds.

The Colts could have collapsed right then—or five minutes later when the Bills came right back to match their first touchdown for a 28-7 second-quarter lead.

Instead they retained their poise and stayed with their game plan. "Even though we were so far behind, we felt, 'Let's go out and play our game,'" Glenn Doughty would relate later. "We stayed with our game plan and with our basic patterns and it just so happened that these patterns attacked the Buffalo defense at its weak points and clicked for big plays."

Just before the half, Marty Domres, the holder, passed fifteen yards for a touchdown to Bill Olds on a fake field goal, and fifty-two seconds later Jones collaborated with Roger Carr on an eighty-nine-yard touchdown pass that tied a club record for distance.

The Colts went off at half time trailing by only 28-21 and they wrapped up the eventual 42-35 victory with twenty-one points in the final period. Carr and Doughty each gained over 100 yards on receptions, Lydell Mitchell scored three touchdowns, and Bert Jones had a spectacular day. He completed fourteen of twenty-two passes for 306 yards and two touchdowns and ran for another score and fifty-nine yards rushing.

This was the greatest comeback in Colts history and it made believers out of a lot of people, not the least of whom were the Baltimore players themselves. George Kunz, as a newcomer with a more detached view than most, could see the team coming together.

The Bills at that point were coming off a 9-5 play-off season and had beaten Baltimore in their first meeting. "Winning this game shows our ball club we can come from behind and beat a good football team," Marchibroda declared. "This is our first big victory and it should help our club greatly. This may be the finest comeback victory I've ever been involved in."

Marchibroda also was ecstatic over Bert's performance, as the young quarterback seemed to be progressing well ahead of schedule. "It was as fine as a quarterback can play in a big game," he said.

Baltimore fans shared the enthusiasm. Some 500 of them were waiting at the airport to greet their returning heroes. A near-sellout crowd of 50,000, the biggest in years, was predicted for the following Sunday at home against the Jets.

From here on, the Colts began to win more and more convincingly. They feasted on their success and drew nourishment from it, driven in large measure by memory of past humiliations.

"Those were terrible years," John Dutton frequently pointed out. "We never want to go back to them."

As the Colts jelled into a winning football team, the first person everyone pointed to was Bert Jones, the quarterback.

Thanks in a major degree to those spring seminars with Marchibroda—and the fact that for the first time in his pro career there was no All-Star game or players' strike to keep him from a full training camp—Bert had matured into a winning quarterback.

It hadn't been easy and it didn't come all at once.

Kunz remembers Bert in the exhibitions and early-season games that same year. "He was shaky," the big tackle pointed out. "You'd get in the huddle and he'd change formations three or four times. 'I-right, no red-right, no brown-right.' You'd think, 'What's going on? Get your formations right.' But it was a learning process for Bert and they put him in there and let him go."

Lydell Mitchell, by now a Colts elder statesman, experienced the same exasperation as Bert kept changing his mind. Many times he was tempted to call a play himself.

"A lot of times Bert would get in a huddle and call a play and change his mind and change his mind again and maybe change it a fourth time. You'd want to scream, 'Hey, man, if you can't think of anything to call, run this.'

"You didn't always agree with his calls then because Bert was involved in a process where you have to have confidence in yourself and the guys around you have to have confidence in you and we didn't have that at first," Mitchell continued. "But now we all have confidence in him. We know he's going to come up with something.

"He started taking charge in '75, maybe not in the beginning of the season, but winning is everything and he got confidence in himself because he was playing well and the team got confidence in him.

"He got to the point where he stepped up and said, 'Okay, guys, I'm running this huddle.' All through my career the quarterback had been captain of the huddle. Unitas was like that. Now it was finally happening with Bert."

"The quarterback has to prove himself before he can get peace in the huddle and Bert had trouble in the beginning," Glenn Doughty says. "The problem was one of confidence and it showed itself in game situations. Being a young quarterback and facing multiple defensive alignments, you've got to second-guess yourself. He might not even have known he was doing that aloud."

Doughty agrees with his teammates that "it all came together in the Buffalo game."

Bert, of course, always knew a quarterback had to take charge of the huddle. He did a lot of yelling at his teammates for mistakes in those early years, they say, but as he gained confidence—and the mistakes became fewer—he became a calmer presence.

One who wasn't surprised at Bert's quick development was John Dutton. "I had played against him in the Orange Bowl and I knew he was going to be a good quarterback. The thing is everyone else had to mature around him as well."

The Colts unanimously credited Marchibroda with sponsoring the sudden improvement of the Colts collectively and Jones individually.

Bert certainly did.

"He was what the team needed and in turn what I needed. I don't throw any better than I did four or five years ago. The difference is mental preparation," Jones said. "I can recognize every defense used against us and I know how to attack it. The reason I'm prepared is Ted Marchibroda.

"I'm not sure he's helped me so much because he used to be a quarterback himself or because he's just a good coach who knows how to get along with people and bring out the best in them. He certainly can prepare a game plan well.

"I feel more comfortable on the field now [because] we've got a new system under Ted—the guy who works the hardest will be the most successful," Bert concluded, and each night the quarterback studied movies that flickered on the wall of his apartment even while he was cooking his own supper. It was hardly the life a swinging bachelor could have enjoyed, but Bert had his priorities fixed. The good times could wait.

Mitchell agreed with Bert's appraisal. "The big change came when Ted Marchibroda came along. He told Bert why he was looking at film and told him what to look for. He told him to be patient, to take his time, take what the defense gives you. Little things like that.

"You could see Bert become a very, very smart quarterback, not just a guy who could drop back and throw the ball," Mitchell continued. "You could see him planning two, three plays ahead."

"I don't think Bert really found out what you had to do to be called a general—which Marty Domres already was—until Ted came here," says Glenn Doughty.

Roger Carr was one of the few Colts who admitted to having enjoyed Thomas's tenure as head coach. After all, Joe had given him a chance to play and his encouragement was a pleasant change from the hostility—real or imagined—he had felt from Schnellenberger. "Joe tried to give us back a little pride," Carr said of the Thomas regime.

The sensitive southerner appreciated Marchibroda's low-key approach. "He's a patient guy," Carr pointed out. "He realized he had a lot of young players like myself. If you sit down with me and talk to me and try to explain things, I'll go out and do my best. Athletes in a way are like kids; they like to be treated reasonably well and if they are, they respond."

Although Marchibroda concentrated mainly on the offense and served as his own offensive coordinator, even the defensive players were impressed by their new coach.

"First of all, we were organized," Stan White said. "We had a system set up that the coaches believed in and that we could adjust to whatever [personnel] we had. Howard came in and tried to put in Miami's system and it didn't work because we didn't have the big fullback and the offensive line to make their ball control offense go. Marchibroda's system could adapt to our personnel. They used a halfback offense in Washington and they were able to do the same here with Lydell.

"We had a system, even defensively, that was sound basic football and not a lot of trick things. We all knew what was going on," continued the articulate linebacker, an off-season law student in Baltimore.

"The difference in the Colts was mainly one of coaching and philosophy because, except for George Kunz, we had pretty much the same personnel. The biggest [individual] change was probably in Bert. Ted taught Bert how to be a quarterback. He gave Bert confidence and that confidence spilled over to the rest of the team," White concluded.

As the Colts started winning, they also began to develop a sense of unity and a team personality. Previously, what little humor there had been on this losing team had come mostly from the sharp-tongued Marty Domres and his practical jokes.

Now the gags began to be heard from different sources. Even Jones got a rise out of Mitchell and some of the other perennial late arrivals in the dressing room by dropping some duck carcasses in their lockers.

The ringleaders, though, were the members of the front four, the merry mastodons, and their guru was Joe Ehrmann. Some people who tried to track him down in off-season referred to the bearded tackle as Gypsy Joe. Privately his teammates call him Rookie, supposedly in honor of a tattoo he bears. Whatever, Joe is the Baltimore Colts' social director.

After a tough game, Ehrmann likes to break the tension before a practice early the next week by slipping his shoulder pads so he resembles the hunchback of Notre Dame. Mike Barnes, known for some reason to his colleagues as Newsboy, his head exotically bandaged, leads Ehrmann out.

The front four gags actually started during the old losing days and the boys think they've tamed their act under Marchibroda's more businesslike regime. But the coach knows what they're up to and watches with detached amusement. "You have to have discipline, but you also have to yield to self-expression. It's like bringing up your children," Marchibroda explains. "The good thing about Joe is that he knows just how far he can go. That's ususual with guys like that, but Joe is very bright, very intelligent.

"I enjoy those guys," Marchibroda says with a smile, "but I enjoy them most when they play football well."

With Lurch (John Dutton) and Cookie Monster (Fred Cook), the front four keep the dressing room alive. Sometimes they'll break into song, a quintet, as trainer Ed Block joins in. Block, perhaps the most beloved member of the Colts family and a welcome guest at players-only parties, can't sing either, but, as Dutton points out, he's also partly deaf so he enjoys what he thinks is harmony.

Ehrmann is the team trivia expert, Dutton the club mimic, and the four guys together are all big enough so nobody risks taking offense when they pin him with a derogative nickname, like, for some reason, The Worm for Mitchell.

Before games, in their nervous energy, the members of the front four find themselves almost unconsciously forming a human chain as they follow each other around the clubhouse. As if by design they will end up in the same corner of the room.

During games they also made arrangements to meet, at the quarterback.

In 1975, they collaborated on tackling the quarterback while passing fifty-nine times, the best record in the league, and that spurred the press to start thinking of a nickname for the unit, something like the Rams' old Fearsome Foursome. Sack Pack seemed to have a nice ring to it, but that was too ordinary for Ehrmann & Co. One day, Joe, relating the group's lunatic antics, was hit with an inspiration. The guys behaved like cartoon characters and seemed to relish their oddball image. Why not Looney Tunes?

Why not, indeed?

The gang often met after the games as well, at parties for the whole team arranged by Joe Ehrmann.

One year Joe masterminded a Roaring Fifties party but his classic efforts are for Hallowe'en. The players usually rent a social room in the suburban apartment complex where many of them live during the season. Bert (Two Beers) Jones and George Kunz skip the costumes and serve as bartenders. Although he's not a big drinker, Bert usually lets go on Hallowe'en among friends. "Last year I brought along a couple of bottles of tequila and Elmer Collett and George

Kunz and I just sort of let the tequila take charge," he remembers with a satisfied smile.

There are prizes for the best costumes, but nobody seems to remember who won.

Some of the costumes are pretty outrageous, as the year Joe Ehrmann showed up as a toilet with the picture of an unnamed Colts authority figure on the seat; or the time Elmer Collett appeared as a mousetrap with live traps fastened all over his shirt ready to spring every time he hugged any of the girls. And he went around hugging the girls.

The best part about the parties was the absence of black/white discrimination. The players, in fact, with their costumes often mocked the racial dissension that split other teams. One year Lloyd Mumphord and Jackie Wallace, the two new boys, showed up as members of the Ku Klux Klan, an organization for which they hardly were eligible for membership. And Mike Barnes once came disguised as Fred Cook, the only black member of the front four, coloring his skin—and riding a tricycle.

The most subtle commentary, though, was provided by Howard and Joyce Stevens, who showed up as "Salt and Pepper." Only Howard, who is black, was "salt" and his white wife was "pepper."

There have been other husband-and-wife combinations. John Dutton came as Dracula, his petite wife as Igor, the hunchback. Last year Joe Ehrmann and his girl friend and huge rookie Ken Novak came as the Flintstone family. Novak, at 6 foot 7 and 275, a "humondous man," according to Bert Jones, was the diapered baby, Bam-Bam.

The most convincing costume may have been Forrest Blue's. He's 6-6, 260, and nicknamed "Tree." So he came as a tree. "He had bamboo shoots stuck all on him and he did look like a potted plant," Jones remembers. "He stood near a corner and I think some people really thought he was a tree or a big plant because they walked around him. Somebody even tried to stand a drink on him." It could have been worse, but there were no dogs at the party.

More solemn is a formal Christmas dinner, not the official function put on by the club after a home game, but a private gathering of players and their families, most of them far away from their own homes on the holidays.

"A lot of the team came up together at the same time," Bert points out. "There are a lot of guys from my draft and the nucleus of the team has been here about the same number of years. We all have the same life-span in Baltimore. We're not established names, just a bunch of kids in the same place playing football."

"If you're all strangers, how can you play together?" John Dutton asks, and as these frisky Colts turned into the home stretch of the 1975 season they were playing better and better.

10
All the Great Ones Are Tough

Yes, the Colts were rolling. They followed their comeback victory over the Bills with a 52-19 rout of the Jets and now their winning streak was at four and they had improved their record to better than .500 for the year.

But an ominous cloud shadowed these victories. Against Buffalo, Bert had been scrambling on a broken play and as he hit the ground the Bills' Vic Washington speared him in the chest with his helmet.

"It was kind of late, but that's irrelevant," Bert says now. "It was just one of those things. He caught me right and things gave."

Bert was obviously in distress when he came off and Ted Marchibroda was concerned. When Baltimore got the ball back, he suggested, "Take a rest. Let Marty go in for this series."

Jones refused. "You're not keeping me out of there," he snarled as he ran back out on the field to direct the Colts' comeback.

Later it was announced that X-rays of Bert's "bruised ribs" were negative.

The quarterback was definitely hurting all the next week

as he prepared to meet the Jets and he played the next two games protected by a thick metal vest that weighed more than four pounds.

This corset actually hindered Jones more than it helped—although you couldn't tell it from the Jets' score—and against Miami he had to leave the game in the second quarter because of it. A hard shot by someone's helmet bent the edge of the vest into Bert's body and reinjured the ribs.

Domres took over for the rest of the game and directed an impressive 33-17 victory that established the Colts as bona fide play-off contenders. Some 10,000 fans greeted the team on its airport arrival from Miami. It seemed like the old days once again when Colts could do no wrong in Baltimore.

The next two weeks, Jones played with no protection, but the injury was aggravated again against the Giants. For the Colts' important rematch against Miami in the next-to-last game of the season, he was fitted with a new lightweight protector made of molded plastic.

Only after the Dolphin game was it disclosed that Bert had actually suffered broken ribs in the Buffalo game. According to the official announcement, the cracks had not shown up in the original X-rays, but a subsequent set of pictures—taken because Jones continued to feel pain—revealed the presence of new calcium growth from the healing process.

It wasn't until after the season that Jones, hinting that the full extent of his injury may have been known to the Colts from the beginning, admitted he had played through most of the season with four ribs broken and cracked in six different places.

"It was just a matter of how long I could go in each game," he said, which gives rise to the suggestion that he also had been given shots of a pain-killer every Sunday. "It was the kind of thing that bugged you each morning and as you walked around the rest of the day. It was all right, except when I had to breathe.

"The offensive line did a super job of keeping 'em off me so I could play through the year, even though I had to leave a few games. It wasn't until the following March before my ribs were completely well."

"When you talk about great quarterbacks, they all have two qualities," Marchibroda says. "Number one is a fine arm, and number two, they have to have great mental and physical toughness. Bert has this. He was hurt, but never to the extent that he couldn't play."

Jones had been hurt while running with the football, a practice even his father had tried to discourage back when Bert was in high school.

"Has anyone tried to discourage me from running? Yes, myself," Jones quips when the subject is raised. "The longevity of the quarterback is directly related to the number of times he gets hit. I'm trying to hold down the running. There is a certain longevity connected with the quarterback job—and I don't want to be the exception."

Because he runs so well, the Colts do have a couple of plays for him in their repertoire, but, Jones says drily, "I'm very conservative about calling my own plays."

Marchibroda is ambivalent about Jones's running with the ball either by design or when pass protection breaks down and he doesn't have time to find an open receiver. "Bert is an excellent runner, not just a running quarterback, and that gives us an added dimension," he points out. But he is also fearful of the damage that can be done to his most irreplaceable performer. "We've talked to him about it but this is one area where he doesn't listen. We don't try to discourage him from running, but we want him to run out of bounds or just fall to the ground when he's going to be hit."

Great players find it difficult to make concessions to caution. Bert is the complete competitor.

"He's thrown seventeen interceptions in the two seasons we've been together and I bet he's made the tackle on sixteen of them," Marchibroda notes with some pride.

Stan White is one of the Colts who marvels at Bert's competitiveness.

"Even when we were losing, he was always out there fighting for everything, just like now. Against Pittsburgh [in the '76 playoffs] Mike Wagner intercepted a pass on him maybe forty yards downfield in the first quarter and yet there was Bert making the tackle before he had gone ten yards the other way. I still don't know how he got all the way downfield to make the tackle.

"He's the same way on fumbles," White continues. "You ought to see him diving in there, ripping the ball away from people even when the play is over. One time at Buffalo, it started to snow just before the half when Bert completed a pass to Doughty and Glenn fumbled after he was hit. Once again, Bert was all the way down there. The play was over and guys are getting up and Bert's still clawing at people trying to get the ball away. Everybody from Buffalo is turning around and looking and saying, 'What's wrong with this guy? Is he nuts or something?' And they started laughing.

"But that's the way he is. When he's out there he has to give 100 percent—or more."

Bert wasn't the only injured Colt as the season turned for home. Mike Curtis, the aggressive linebacker, had hurt his knee in training camp, but not badly enough to require immediate surgery. Still, the knee wasn't getting any better and it appeared to be hampering his performance. On top of this, he was not getting along with Marchibroda. The defense Ted and Maxie Baughan had brought from Washington is highly disciplined and cerebral. Curtis had always played instinctively and with reckless abandon. Since he had been so successful over the years, he saw no reason to change.

When Curtis suffered an eye injury against the Patriots early in the season, it gave Marchibroda an opportunity to start Jim Cheyunski in Mike's middle linebacker spot. The former Buffalo veteran played well, and even after Curtis's eye healed he continued to start. The demotion did not sit well with Curtis, one of only a handful of Colts left from the previous regime. Always outspoken, he became even more of a vocal presence in the locker room. Marchibroda wondered about his influence on the younger players and confided this concern to Joe Thomas. Eventually, it was decided that since Mike wasn't going to be playing that much the rest of the season anyway, they might as well operate on his knee to give it more time to heal for the following campaign.

Few doubted that Curtis would be playing elsewhere in 1976, but the circumstances of his eventual departure would prove traumatic for the franchise.

Despite these difficulties and Bert's broken ribs, the Colts kept winning. They shut out the Giants, 21-0, to make it seven in a row for an 8-4 record, and now they trailed the Dolphins by only a single game in the Eastern Division standings. Miami was coming up to Baltimore that Sunday for the Colts' most important game in many years.

This game was especially critical because in case of an eventual tie in the standings, Baltimore would be awarded the championship if the Colts could show two regular-season victories over the Dolphins. But they had to win. Even a tie would clinch the championship for Miami and eliminate Baltimore from any chance of making the play-offs.

For some weeks the Colts had been speculating about their chances of making the play-offs. Suddenly what had started out as the wildest fantasy became a distinct possibility. And it was all in their hands. "Do or die," Bert said, "because if we only tie, we lose."

As usual on game days, Jones rose early. Hunters, farmers, and pilots all check the weather first thing on rising and Bert qualified on all three counts. He could tell it was going to be "a sloppy day." How sloppy, though, even Bert couldn't guess. By the second half, a heavy fog settled over Memorial Stadium. You could not see from one end zone to the other. Even Bert's ducks and geese would have been grounded.

Marchibroda's pregame pep talk was low-keyed and businesslike as usual. "Nothing could have been said that was not known in everybody's mind and heart," Bert recalls. "It was a very key game and really the whole season. Sure, we were going to have a winning season, but that wouldn't mean anything to me or to all the ball players if we lost this game. Ted just reiterated the fact that this was a big game."

The first half was scoreless, but late in the third quarter Miami jumped ahead when Mercury Morris circled left end from the three and Garo Yepremian converted for a 7-0 lead. The Colts' first sellout crowd in more than two years, numbering almost 60,000, sat in silence as if the fog had muffled all sound from the audience.

However, halfway through the final period, Jones finally got the Colts moving. With time now a factor, he directed a twelve-play, eighty-six-yard drive that was climaxed when Lydell Mitchell followed a George Kunz block to score from the six. Toni Linhart converted for a 7-7 tie with 5½ minutes to go.

Neither team was able to score during that period, but the Colts still had another chance to avoid the eliminating tie. The game now went into overtime, a recent innovation by the league for regular-season games. It's sudden death, meaning first team to score by any means wins, but they play only a single fifteen-minute quarter. If neither team scores in that time, the game is declared a draw.

There is a new coin toss for the overtime and the Dolphins, division winners for the last four years and twice Super Bowl champions, won to get the critical first possession. They were unable to score, but Coach Don Shula was not concerned, especially when punter Larry Seiple got off a perfect coffin-corner kick out of bounds at the Baltimore four.

Even a safety wins in sudden death and that was now a possibility. In any case, the Colts would have to drive ninety-six yards to score and Shula was confident his defense would respond. If they held early and forced Baltimore to punt from its end zone, Miami would set up again close to field goal position.

The Colts got one first down, but Shula's confidence increased when Baltimore found itself third-and-fifteen at its own nineteen after Jones had been sacked for a ten-yard loss. This could be the biggest play of the game and Bert pondered what to call.

He knew the Dolphins would not risk getting beaten by one long bomb and so would be concentrating on his deep receivers. That would probably leave single coverage on Raymond Chester, the Colts' tight end and a dangerous pass receiver. In the huddle, Bert called a simple "out" pattern for Chester. Normally the pattern is run ten or twelve yards deep, but this time the Colts needed more to assure the first down. "Stretch it out," Bert told Chester as the huddle broke and the experienced tight end knew he had to "go for the sticks," the sideline marker that showed how much he needed for a first down.

As the play developed, Jones read the Dolphins going into the coverage he had anticipated. Chester is 6-4, 236, fast, and smart, and he was covered one-on-one by the strong safety, who had no outside help. Chester broke for the sidelines, got open, and Jones hit him for a seventeen-yard gain that kept the drive going.

Twice more during the march, Jones passed to Roger Carr for short gains. Bert's nature was to send Carr deep so he could send the customers home in a hurry with a dazzling long bomb for the winning score. But on this day he muzzled his gambling instincts. Delicately he carved Miami's defense, a snip here, a slice there. Four times he had to make good on third-down plays to keep possession.

Finally, as the Colts moved across the fifty into field goal range, Bert switched to safe running plays, seven of them in a row. On third-and-five from the Miami sixteen, Jones kept the football himself so as not to risk a fumble on the hand-off, and he dove to the ground after gaining two yards.

Now it was fourth down at the fourteen and Toni Linhart walked out on the field with Marty Domres to hold for him.

Bert came off and virtually collapsed on the sidelines. The game had lasted longer than anticipated and whatever pain-killers Jones had taken had long since worn off. On top of this he had been tackled with the ball three times on this drive. He was in agony. Each breath, each movement sent jagged arrows of pain through his rib cage. He knelt on the sidelines trying to hold himself together as trainers nervously hovered around him. He could go no further.

Marchibroda, meanwhile, huddled with Stan White, leader of the defense. A coach must be prepared. He was reminding White that if Linhart missed, the Dolphins still would have time to go on the offensive themselves. Even though Miami might want to play it safe for a tie, the Colts had to try to get the ball back. "Remember, we've still got two time-outs," he told his linebacker.

The conversation was needless. With 2:16 left in the overtime, Toni Linhart kicked a thirty-one-yard field goal that won the game, 10-7.

"Give the game ball to Bert Jones," said the downhearted Dolphins.

The victory was tremendously satisfying for Ted Marchibroda. He had taken on Bert Jones as his personal protege and on this foggy afternoon he had seen the young quarterback suddenly become "thirty years of age," as he knew he would eventually have to do to win this kind of game.

"Bert has had games where he's thrown for more yardage, but the Miami game was by far the best he's had from a standpoint of play-calling, even though his play-calling has been excellent all season," Marchibroda said.

The coach was especially pleased because in the ball-control drives leading to both Baltimore scores, Jones showed enough self-discipline to go "against all his natural instincts."

Marchibroda explained: "It's Bert's style to go for the big play, to try to bomb the opposition. But he knew exactly what he had to do to beat Miami and he did it. He picked them apart with good plays—four yards here, five yards there —never doing anything that could kill the drive. It was a masterpiece of work both times."

Marchibroda had been watching the blackboard quarterback come to life just as he had been programmed the past spring. One situation still comes to mind.

"We're in the last quarter and the score is 7-7 and Bert came to me on the sidelines and asked, 'Coach, am I doing the right thing?' Well, as long as we're 7-7 with Miami in

1975, I know we're doing the right thing, so I said, 'Yeah, Bert, everything's going fine,' " Marchibroda related recently.

"I think what he was talking about was the fact that we had been backed up in our own territory the entire second half and we were playing it pretty safe, we weren't taking any chances. This is what I felt he was asking about.

"I knew he had talked about this sort of thing during those six weeks in the winter and spring and they were having a direct effect on the ball game," Marchibroda continued. "We had talked about situations where the thing was not to go out to try to win all of a sudden, but to make sure you didn't do anything to lose it. Right then I felt those meetings had been fruitful even if this was the only thing we got out of it.

"This was the one ball game where Bert became the total quarterback. I felt that in this game he played like a thirty-year-old quarterback—and he has continued to play that way."

The Colts enjoyed what Jones classifies as a "mild" victory celebration after beating Miami, but they were still not assured of making the play-offs. They were tied in the standings with the Dolphins but each team had one more game to play.

Late in the season, when the college schedule is completed, the NFL plays some games on Saturday. Thus the Dolphins set the task squarely in front of Baltimore by winning their last game a day early, 14-13, over Denver. The Colts finished up the following afternoon at home against New England.

The Patriots were closing with a dismal 3-10 record but they showed plenty of character and promise for the future in what for them was a meaningless game. They stunned the home team early when Allen Carter returned the opening kickoff ninety-nine yards for a 7-0 advantage and subsequently held leads of 14-10 and 21-20. The Colts didn't wrap up their 34-21 victory until Nelson Munsey returned a Steve Grogan interception thirty yards for a touchdown in the fourth quarter and in the last minute Stan White set an NFL record for linebackers with his eighth interception of the season. Not bad for the somewhat undersized seventeenth-round draft choice who thinks the only reason he got a real chance in his first training camp was because Don McCafferty had coached for years at Kent State University and so knew Stan as a hometown boy from Kent, Ohio.

Now the Colts could really celebrate their first division title since 1970.

This 2-and-12 team had totally turned around in a single year. Winning their last nine games for a 10-4 record, the Colts were in the play-offs!

A grim landscape greeted the Colts when they got to Pittsburgh the following week for their first-round game. Pittsburgh can be a tough, forbidding city, especially in December, and so is its football team. The Steelers, always dangerous at home, were defending Super Bowl champions and confident they could win it again.

It was cold in Three Rivers Stadium. It snowed heavily before the game but quit in time for the kickoff except for a few brief flurries as the game progressed.

Jones had studied hard. He knew he was prepared for the best effort of his young career. But on the fourth play of the game his high hopes shattered in an explosion of pain. Bert was running with the ball and ducked to the ground as he was about to be tackled. J. T. Thomas, the Pittsburgh cornerback, tried to avoid hitting the prone quarterback, but as he leaped over Jones his knee hit Bert in the back of the right arm in the triceps muscle.

"My arm kind of exploded like a balloon filled with water," Bert says. All the fluid settled in his elbow and he found he could not bend his arm. The whole arm, except for a spot in his palm, turned black like a huge bruise. It was an ugly injury, not really painful but totally disabling. Bert could not go back in the game. A freak injury, not even related to his rib problem, in Bert's words "handcuffed" him to the sideline.

Marty Domres, whose practice time had been limited during the week because of a minor injury, had to take over. He didn't do badly at first, turning a 7-0 Baltimore deficit into a 10-7 lead, but the Steelers in turn rallied for a 21-10 advantage in the fourth quarter.

Jones seethed in frustration on the sidelines. Time and again he and Marchibroda checked with each other. Each time Bert had to respond with a negative shake of his head. He simply could not throw the football.

Finally, though, only one quarter remained to be played, possibly the final quarter of Baltimore's season. Bert at last was able to get some flexion in his elbow. "Looks like this is it," Marchibroda said and this time Bert nodded, "Yes." He could give it a try.

Somehow, Jones was able to rally the Colts. In the closing minutes he drove them down to Pittsburgh's three. But then he was tackled by Jack Ham, fumbled, and Andy Russell picked up the loose ball and ran ninety-three yards for the wrap-up touchdown in a 28-10 Steeler victory.

Pittsburgh went on to win its second straight Super Bowl.

The Colts paused to assess their final loss and the fairy-tale season.

"It was awfully hard to expect to win when your No. 1 gun is out," Marchibroda said. "It hurt to lose Bert so early and you couldn't expect Marty Domres, who hadn't played all year, to beat Pittsburgh. You've got to be sharp and trained and honed to play in a ball game like that and it wasn't Marty's fault that we lost." Earlier, he had considerately told Domres the same thing in the privacy of the locker room.

As for Jones, the quarterback said defiantly, "We'll be back. We didn't win our division on luck, we worked real hard and studied and executed to get where we got. Our players are all maturing together and we will work harder. We should be stronger simply because we will know more. With a little more maturity and maybe some help, we'll be back."

On his way out of the stadium, Jones paused briefly to talk privately with his coach. He thanked Marchibroda for all he had done to make him a better quarterback and then he asked for one more favor. "When you grade the films after the season, critique my performance very thoroughly. Let me know what's still needed."

11
Shake and Bake

Bert Jones had plenty on his mind besides the Colts' internal bickering after the 1975 season.

He sold his interest in the restaurant in Aspen, he wheeled and dealed with some property—and he got well. It took some three weeks for the discoloration to leave his injured arm and several months for the ribs to fully heal, which set back his off-season conditioning program a bit.

There also was the matter of a new contract. Bert's rookie deal with the Colts was expiring and 1976 would mark his option year, if he chose to play it that way. With the Rozelle Rule suspended—temporarily as it turned out—by court order, Bert could have played the 1976 season for 90 percent of his previous salary, become a free agent, and then held a sky's-the-limit auction for his services.

But that's not the Jones family style and, besides, Bert did not want to be hassled by the media as to his intentions all through the next season.

He and Joe Thomas sat down and hammered out a new five-year agreement.

During the term of the new contract, Bert's salary would escalate from approximately $185,000 annually to about $310,000, easily a million-dollar package.

Bert may have been happy with the agreement, but Joe Thomas was ecstatic. That's because there was no signing bonus, which Bert might have demanded; a minimum of incentive bonuses; and, except for injury protection through the life of the agreement, nothing was guaranteed.

Thomas thus was able to hold to his personal ban on no-cut contracts and he could point out to others who sought them that even the Colts' best player didn't have a guaranteed deal.

Bert negotiated the contract himself and then had his brother, the lawyer, look it over. No agent skimmed 10 percent or more off the top.

Jones won't discuss the terms in detail, but he says contentedly, "It's a lot of money, for sure."

Bert thinks football players, and all athletes, may be overpaid these days. "It's just ridiculous," he says, "but it's all relative and if they get it, I need to get it, too—and maybe even a little more 'cause I'm better."

This last is spoken with a little-boy grin, but confidence is really the basis of Bert's agreement with the Colts.

"Look, I don't want a no-cut contract because I'm going to be good enough to play for five years," he insists. "The only thing that would keep me from it is injury and then I'd be paid anyway, so what's the need in it? If I quit, I don't want them to have to pay me, and if they fire me, which I don't think they'd do, then I don't deserve to be paid."

As for incentive clauses, Bert says, "All my money is real money. I don't want to feel I have to complete a certain number of passes to get paid."

Bert in 1975 had completed 59 percent of his passes for eighteen touchdowns with only eight interceptions as the fourth best passer in the NFL. Old neighbors Terry Bradshaw, Joe Ferguson, and James Harris all were strung out behind him. Ted Marchibroda had called him "at this stage ahead of Gabriel, Jurgensen, and Kilmer," the previous big three in his personal book. Yes, Jones had plenty of reason to feel good as the 1976 season approached.

Still, every star needs to learn a little humility and Bert got a small measure that summer when he came up to New York with Colts PR director Barry Jones for Old-Timers Day at Yankee Stadium. Ernie Accorsi, then working for the NFL between hitches in the Colts' front office, accompanied them as Jones thrilled while legendary names from baseball's past were introduced in the newly refurbished but still historic ball park.

Later Accorsi took them to a small Italian restaurant he had discovered in midtown New York.

As they strolled down somewhat seedy Ninth Avenue, a neighborhood derelict turned away from his wine bottle and gave them a double take.

"Hey, I know you," he said staring at Bert. "You're—you're —you're Kyle Rote, Jr.!"

"Yeah, I guess we could be look-alikes," Jones grumbles when reminded of the story. Apparently he had been confused with the pro soccer star before.

When the Colts reported to training camp, they discovered someone had posted in their dressing room a stark reminder of what they still had to accomplish. Hanging side by side were two Colts' football schedules. On the left was the 1975 card with scores filled in for fifteen games. Pointedly left blank were the results of the American Conference championship game and the Super Bowl. On the right was a virginal 1976 schedule with seventeen spaces to be completed. The season would be dedicated to filling in all the blanks this time.

The Colts opened their season in New England and it

might have been easy to overlook the Patriots, who were coming off a 3-11 record. But the turmoil of the previous week had given all the Baltimore players extra resolve. "It's kind of like the Super Bowl today," Jones declared.

Marchibroda also reminded them of how tough the Patriots had been in their season-ending game the year before.

The Patriots were just as rambunctious this time. Baltimore jumped off to a 3-0 lead, but then New England went in front, 6-3, on a pair of John Smith field goals. The Colts didn't take command until Jones completed a pair of touchdown passes to Glenn Doughty in a span of forty-one seconds in the last minute of the first half. Overall, Bert was 17 for 22 passing in the 27-13 victory.

After the game the Colts handed out four game balls and there was special significance in two of them that went to Marchibroda and Maxie Baughan, the defensive coordinator who had turned down a chance to be head coach. On the playing side, one ball went to Jackie Wallace, the slender free safety who intercepted three passes, and the other was presented to Joe Ehrmann. Despite a severe headache from the previous week's concussion, Ehrmann played a whale of a game against the Pats until he was kayoed again in the closing minutes.

Bob Irsay did not come down on the field or visit the dressing room after this victory, and players reacted with sarcastic derision when asked if the owner would have received a game ball, too, if he had showed.

Jim Cheyunski, who excelled at middle linebacker despite a painful and swollen knee that had to be drained regularly of excess fluid, summed up the feeling of the Colts.

"We knew we had to win," he declared. "We felt a lot of pressure and the guys came in sighing with relief that it was over. It felt like a big weight off our shoulders. The recent

problems weren't mentioned by anyone before the game. Nobody had to mention it. We all knew what we had to do.
What went on was just unbelievable, but we got the coach
back. It lifted us. It fired us up."

Meanwhile, Marchibroda told those reporters who asked
in the dressing room that Irsay was "welcome here any
time."

The owner took him up on it the following Sunday after
the Colts' home opener against the dangerous Cincinnati
Bengals, although for most of the game he couldn't be certain whether he would be visiting a winning or a losing
clubhouse.

With Jones throwing three first-half interceptions, the
Colts trailed 17-7 in the second period, 20-14 at the half, and
27-21 in the third quarter. However, a two-yard touchdown
plunge by Roosevelt Leaks in the fourth period finally gave
the home team a 28-27 victory.

After his early problems, Jones was devastating against
the Bengals, passing for 301 yards and three touchdowns
covering 68, 22, and 65 yards. All of these went to Roger
Carr, and to Marchibroda this was a good sign. With virtually the same personnel returning and with Jones already at
the top of his game mechanically, Marchibroda knew that
any improvement in the Colts' offense for 1976 would have
to be provided by Roger Carr.

In 1975 Roger had caught only two touchdown passes.
Perhaps it was added confidence and maturity or perhaps it
was off-season drills with Bert Jones, who would fly to Cotton Valley to pick him up, but Carr in 1976 developed into
one of the best deep receivers in football. He ended up the
season with eleven touchdown catches and a dazzling 25.9-
yard average for each of his forty-three receptions.

The third Sunday of the season, the Colts moved down to

Dallas for a shootout with the Cowboys, and that's just what it was as these two play-off contenders combined for twenty-three points in the final quarter. Spectators knew that whichever team had the ball last would win. Jones was 13 of 31 for 237 yards and he ran for one touchdown. Roger Staubach of the Cowboys was even more spectacular. He completed twenty-two of twenty-eight for 339 yards and two TDs.

In the end, though, it came down to the two immigrant place-kickers. Austrian Toni Linhart booted a twenty-four-yard field goal to haul the Colts into a 27-27 tie with twenty-eight seconds left in the fourth period, but then Mexican-born Efren Herrera retaliated with a thirty-two yarder with only three ticks left for a 30-27 Dallas decision.

"We didn't really lose, we were just behind when time ran out," Jones stated glumly.

Still, the Colts were 2 and 1 after the tough opening portion of their schedule and Marchibroda was far from displeased.

"I didn't tell you this before, but that's the goal I set for us before the season," the coach disclosed. "After three games, we're right on schedule."

During this period Marchibroda unveiled a new offensive wrinkle he would use for the rest of the season with considerable success.

In Don McCauley, the Colts owned a versatile running back who could play either halfback or fullback. At 215 pounds, he had 20 pounds on Mitchell and he was a much better receiver than Leaks. McCauley had been a regular in past seasons and Marchibroda did not want him to feel he had been completely discarded.

As a solution, Marchibroda decided to use McCauley as a situation substitute. On passing downs, third-and-long, McCauley would replace the iron-handed, lead-footed Leaks as an extra receiver. Since Mitchell excelled in that area, the Colts would have two dangerous pass catchers coming out of the backfield and because of Jones's mobility it was not as necessary to keep one or both in to block. On third-and-short, or whenever the Colts got down on the goal line, McCauley also came in, but for Mitchell. Leaks weighed 225 and he and McCauley provided plenty of beef when the Colts only needed a couple of yards against a tightly massed defense.

Mitchell for a while may have resented the fact that his touchdown totals dropped way down, but he eventually realized what Marchibroda was doing to keep McCauley involved and contributing. More important to Mitchell, McCauley's presence was saving a lot of wear and tear on his body. It gets pretty rough down on the goal line and there are few places a halfback can go to escape being hit. Mitch would still get his 1,000 yards but pay less of a physical price.

By season's end, the stat sheet showed McCauley as the Colts' third leading ground-gainer, fourth leading pass receiver, and second leading scorer with eleven touchdowns.

Marchibroda came up with another innovation to improve morale, this one off the field. He called it Monday Afternoon Football, a play on the nighttime series on ABC that had helped make Howard Cosell a household name.

In this case, it also could have been called Monday Afternoon at the Movies. The Colts would gather as a team in a large classroom to go over films of their game the previous day. If they had won—as they usually did—they could really enjoy the sessions as coaches pointed out Sunday's heroes.

"The only thing missing was popcorn and cokes," one player noted and the whole thing was carried off with enthusiasm and good humor.

Marchibroda had the front office contact Baltimore merchants about donating prizes for his players and so restaurant meals, gasoline, front-end alignments, TV sets, and barbecue grills were awarded to the various stars each week. There was always a prize for the player who had excelled on special teams.

Joe Ehrmann then would take over to present his personal Bonehead of the Week Award to whoever made the most embarrassing play of the game. This award, of course, was always accompanied by hoots and jeers from the audience.

At the end of the season, Ehrmann presented his Bonehead of the Year Award for the season's most embarrassing moment.

This prize in '76 was given to Roosevelt Leaks, the short yardage specialist, who had a chance to score on a fifty-yard run but fell down without being touched ten yards from the goal when his leg cramped up on him. There had been no Buffalo player within yards of him at the time.

For his performance, Leaks received a regular, formal trophy. But instead of the usual replica of Victory stretching her arms skyward atop the pedestal, there was the perfectly sculpted rear end of a horse.

"A thing like this, it helped keep us together," Roger Carr pointed out.

The Ehrmann-Marchibroda awards sessions weren't the only togetherness clinics on the Colts.

Glenn Doughty had his own little morale-booster called Shake and the Bakers and it was, yes, a players' rock group.

Starting halfway through the 1975 season, Doughty had made "Shake and Bake" his personal rallying cry.

"As I run my pattern, I give the cornerback a shake. Then I either go into my pattern or I go by him and I bake him— and that means he's cooked," Doughty explains.

"The next thing I knew, this thing caught on with the rest

of the offense, and then the defense, and soon the whole team was shakin' and bakin'."

Doughty writes and performs radio and television commercials for a Baltimore firm in the off-season and soon he was composing little jingles for each opponent, all with the shake and bake theme, as:

"We're gonna shake and bake some Dolphin steak/With a funky feeling we're gonna leave Miami reeling."

Or:

"We're gonna shake and bake some Buffalo meat/We're gonna put Buffalo in the oven and give 'em no lovin'."

It may not have been Ogden Nash (the late humorous poet, from Baltimore, was a big Colts fan), but it struck a note with Doughty's teammates. Later he composed a melody to go with these lyrics, and following their 33-17 rout of the Dolphins, the Colts were "shakin' and bakin' " all the way home on their chartered plane. Reporters with their tape recorders captured this magic moment and area disc jockeys, who had access to the tapes, played it often.

During the off-season, Doughty got his song copyrighted and when training camp began he talked up the idea of forming a musical group among the players. Anything to break the training camp monotony, he reasoned, although by the end of the year some of his teammates wished he had taken a different route.

Doughty himself was the lead singer and played the congas. Raymond Chester was on bass, Lloyd Mumphord, a pretty good musician, played harmonica, and Freddie Scott performed with the percussion or cymbals.

For lead guitar, the Colts could thank Joe Thomas for signing a free agent defensive back out of Canada named David (D. T.) White. "D. T. played a mean lead guitar," Doughty says.

Still, something was missing. The group needed one more instrument for just the right sound. A friend told Doughty he knew a drummer, a shoe salesman named Bruce Barnett, who would love to sit in with the football players.

"Send him over to my house tonight 'cause we're practicing and we'll give him a shot," Doughty replied, and Barnett showed up with his drums and he fit right in.

"You got it, man; you with us," Doughty told him and the Bakers was complete.

The group was filmed in action at the Colts' annual Hallowe'en party—some of the square Colts confess they sneaked off to Bert Jones's apartment to rest their ears with some country and western music—and from there the Bakers caught on in Baltimore.

With some lead-in assistance from Chuck Thompson, radio voice of the Colts, the Bakers cut a record and as the team continued to win, managers of clubs around Baltimore discovered the Bakers were good for business. The Bakers, of course, loved the exposure and now other players wanted to get into the act.

"Everybody wanted to tinkle on something or sing or play the flute," Doughty grumbled.

Lydell Mitchell was allowed in and he did some singing—"Or tried to sing," says Doughty—and played percussion, but he seldom showed up for rehearsals. Because of that he was benched for the recording session.

As far as the Bakers were concerned, the Colts went through two major crises in training camp. One was keeping Ted Marchibroda as coach, the other involved keeping D. T. White as lead guitar. Retaining D. T., a mere 5-11, 175-pounder who had flunked a previous trial with the Bills, was by far the more difficult.

D. T. could play the guitar more than well enough to make

the group; the question was whether he could play football well enough to make the team. Onstage, he was the Bakers' star; on the gridiron, well, he was just another free agent with a minimal chance of making the team.

In fact, the Colts thought so little of his prospects that when they prepared their preliminary roster for training camp he was assigned jersey No. 98, the only one of twelve defensive backs not given a number that fit the position.

Still, he managed to hang on until late in training camp when he was injured. Gloom on the Bakers. A minor injury was a preliminary to being cut.

But it was a knee injury, a serious knee injury. Gloom turned to gladness. You can't cut a player while he's hurt and D. T. figured to be hurt for a while. When the Colts put White on their injured reserve list, which meant they had written him off for the year, his musical teammates were overjoyed. That meant he would be on the payroll and on the bandstand the rest of the season.

But, alas, two weeks from the end of the season, D. T. showed up with a sad look on his face. His knee had healed and the team was able to put him on waivers. Joe Thomas had just called to say he was being released. More gloom among the Bakers until their lead guitar promised to stay around for the rest of the season. Sheer joy.

But short-lived. Now D. T. called to say the Green Bay Packers wanted to sign him up. The Bakers were desolate. Their lead guitar not only would have to leave but if he froze his fingers in Green Bay he might never play again.

At last, though, a happy ending. The Packers told D. T. he would not have to report until the following spring.

For as far as the Colts went in the season and in the play-offs, the Bakers would not have to make it without their splendid lead guitar.

Doughty had grandiose plans of getting the Bakers on national television, but the Colts slumped slightly near the end of the season and these dreams, like some others, had to be deferred.

"Shake and Bake" also was put on an eight-track tape and this is where the Colts' precious team unity underwent its most severe trial.

The one-melody number was repeated endlessly in the locker room and there developed almost open warfare between the Bakers and their partisans who loved the tune and the rest of the Colts who preferred something else—anything else.

As one teammate who had best be kept anonymous critiqued, "Mumphord's the best on his harmonica and the rest of them play instruments and sing, if that's what you want to call it. They're not real good, but they try hard and they believe in themselves. People seem to enjoy them and that's what's important."

Although he concedes, "It was just good criticism from teammates," Doughty was learning how an artist often must suffer for his muse. "Oh, man, I took a lot of flak from the guys," he says, "I had to develop alligator skin."

Actually, "alligator skin" is appropriate armor for any wide receiver. Defensive backs traditionally try to intimidate pass catchers, verbally and physically, although the talkative Doughty dishes out a lot more than he receives in the words department. Glenn Edwards, Pittsburgh's rawhide free safety, in fact, calls Doughty "Muhammad Ali" after another famous motor-mouth.

Doughty learned his motto had become famous when Edwards warned him before the 1975 play-off game, "Muhammad, you're not going to shake and bake here today." Doughty got the second laugh when he caught a touchdown pass from Marty Domres and told Edwards in the end zone, "Well, here I am and I'm gonna be here all day." But the scoreboard gave Edwards and the rest of the Steelers the final chuckle.

The most important thing was that Shake and the Bakers never lost sight of the real purpose of their group. While they were jiving and being jived by their unappreciative teammates, they were doing it all together, and with a smile.

"After we'd win, we'd chant 'Shake and Bake' and it was a good thing for the team and it helped bring us and the town together," Doughty points out.

After their loss to Dallas, the Colts took on the state of Florida and thrashed Tampa Bay and Miami on successive weeks. This marked their third straight victory over the once-haughty Dolphins and John Dutton crowed, "They're going down and we're just rising."

"No question, the Colts are in the driver's seat," Don Shula agreed as he surveyed the division standings.

After two more one-sided victories over the state of New York, meaning Buffalo and the Jets, Jones said confidently, "The team to beat is us."

With four straight victories for a 6-1 record, the Colts entered the second half of their schedule with a Monday nighter against the Oilers at home. The Oilers had not been playing well, but they were a physically tough team and their chances looked a lot better when Bert Jones showed up at the stadium deathly ill. Bert had been sick with the flu since Friday and spent most of the weekend trying to hold down some nourishment despite nausea and a fever that reached as high as 103 degrees.

"There sure was a lot of question about me playing," Bert says, but Marchibroda insists such a possibility of not playing him "never entered our minds."

The shaky and pale quarterback managed to cram down the pregame meal about five o'clock Monday evening, but threw it up before the kickoff. He got sick again on the sidelines during the first quarter but forced himself to run around a bit and, oddly, the fever broke.

Despite his illness, Bert enjoyed one of his finest games before the national TV audience, completing nineteen of twenty-eight passes for 197 yards.

Lydell Mitchell also had a big game with 136 yards on twenty-eight carries, and after the 38-14 rout he passed Bob Irsay in the locker room. "When are you going to start playing?" Irsay asked with a deadpan expression.

Did he truly not recognize Mitchell or was this a put-on relating to his tirade back in preseason?

Mitchell couldn't be sure. He introduced himself anew to his boss with a similar blank expression. "I'm Lydell Mitchell."

"I know, I know," Irsay insisted and hugged the little man about the neck.

"Now I know how the Rebels felt when they came marching north," said Bum Phillips, the shaken Oilers coach.

The Colts ran their winning streak to six by beating the Chargers as San Diego coach Tommy Prothro raved, "I have never been as impressed with a quarterback as I was with Bert Jones," but then they faltered.

The roadblock was thrown up by the emerging New England Patriots. Jones hurt a finger on his passing hand as the nail was ripped off and did not enjoy a good day. The Pats won, 21-14. The loss dropped Baltimore to an 8-2 record, best in the American Conference-East but only a single game ahead of the surprising Pats.

Some ten weeks earlier Irsay had blessed out his coach and players for losing. On this occasion he made it a point to publicly encourage Marchibroda for a good job.

Up in New England, Chuck Fairbanks also was doing a pretty fine job with a once-dormant franchise, and the following Sunday the Pats cut Baltimore's lead to a mere half game by routing the Jets, 38-24.

The Colts, not scheduled until Monday night in Miami, thus knew they had to win to keep the Patriots behind them. In many ways, the Pats reminded them of themselves a year ago, young and hungry and just beginning to feel their power. With a little encouragement, the Pats could be dangerous. They could not be allowed to catch up.

The Dolphins were dangerous, too. Decimated by two years of injuries and defections, they were about to present Don Shula with the first losing season of his coaching career. He would not take that lightly. Playing at home in the Orange Bowl, the Dolphins could be formidable, like the old fighter who can't move but still knows how to punch.

As the game began, the Colts seemed comfortably in control, as befits a team en route to the play-offs. They led 14-3 in the second quarter and 17-10 late in the fourth.

But as the clock wound down, the Colts seemed to lose something. Miami put a heavy rush on Jones and the Baltimore quarterback was harried out of his plan and his poise. Not only was he sacked five times, but on seven other occasions he was forced to run with the ball when his protection broke down before he could find a receiver.

On one play, Bert's temper exploded, one of the few times it has ever happened publicly. The Colts for this game had put in a special quick screen pass that involved Lydell Mitchell going in motion. Down on the Dolphin four, Bert called the play and when he dropped back he saw there was nobody from Miami in position to defend against it. Unfortunately, Mitchell not only had lined up on the wrong side, he went in motion in the wrong direction. Jones, under heavy pressure from Randy Crowder and Bob Matheson of the Dolphins, looked for the halfback and he wasn't there. The Dolphin rush hit him and he fumbled and the Colts lost a chance to score. Afterwards fans in the Orange Bowl and especially on national television, which zoomed in for a closeup, could see Bert berating his teammate, who earlier in the game had just gone over 1,000 yards rushing for the season.

This error proved critical because it prevented Baltimore from putting the game out of reach. As the scoreboard clock ticked down, Bob Griese of the Dolphins showed some of his old fourth-quarter magic by driving Miami to another touchdown that cut Baltimore's lead to a single point.

Only twelve seconds remained when Garo Yepremian came on the field to attempt the extra point that would tie the game.

On the sidelines, Jones huddled with Marchibroda. They were discussing their strategy for the probable overtime. How often does anyone miss an extra point? "Make sure they go over the ground rules again," Marchibroda warned his quarterback.

But even as they spoke, defensive tackle Mike Barnes broke through to block Yepremian's kick with his outstretched right thumb.

Don Shula was still protesting the officials' invalidation of Miami's apparent recovery of the ensuing onside kick when time ran out on Baltimore's 17-16 victory.

There were two interesting elements in the decisive blocked PAT.

On Miami's side, a guard, Bob Keuchenberg, normally centered the ball on punts and place kicks. He just happened to be good at it. But this night Keuchenberg was sidelined with bone chips in his ankle. Jim Langer had to take over for the long snap and his effort on this kick was a trifle high.

Earl Morrall, the holder, had to reach up about a foot and the split second or so it took him to pull the ball down threw off Yepremian's timing. That's one of the reasons his kick was somewhat low.

As for Barnes, he was only dimly aware of his heroic achievement in the stadium where he had played college ball for the University of Miami. He uses one of those air suspension helmets in which a cushion of air protects the head, but the helmet sprung a leak and he suffered a concussion early in the game.

Ed Block, the trainer and den mother of all the Colts but especially the defensive line, kept a close watch on Barnes on the sidelines after he had been taken from the lineup. But as the game progressed, other injured players required Block's ministrations. Unattended for the moment, Barnes charged out on the field for the next series. He played by memory for a while before the team doctors noticed his presence on the field and ordered him off again.

Only much later was he deemed sound enough to return to the game, and he made the play that won it.

To Marchibroda, this was the victory that put Baltimore, in his words, "over the hump." True, they led New England by only one game with three to play, but two of these were at home against comparatively weak opponents, the Jets and Buffalo. In between there was a nonconference excursion to St. Louis.

The Colts knew they had a virtual lock on the play-offs and, despite a loss to the Cardinals, they routed the Jets and Bills for an 11-3 record and a second straight Eastern Division championship.

Once again the Colts were matched against Pittsburgh in the first round of the play-offs, but this time they would get the Steelers at home, in friendly Memorial Stadium with perhaps the worst grass (or dirt) field in pro football—"Astro-dirt," the Colts call it—and easily the best (and loudest) set of fans supporting the home team.

There was another switch to the pairing. A year ago the Colts had been forced to win their last nine games to make the play-offs. One slip and they were out. The Steelers had cruised into the postseason parade with a 12-2 record en route to their second straight Super Bowl triumph.

This time it was the Colts who had been in front all the way, the Steelers who had to struggle. The defending champions had lost four of their first five games but then had rallied for nine straight victories behind the greatest defensive display in league history to make the play-offs on the last week of the season.

"We've got a lot of things going for us," Marchibroda figured as he privately analyzed the upcoming game. "We knew we were going to be in the play-offs from the twelfth game of the season and that helps us. The previous year we had to win nine straight to get in there and as I told our team after we lost in the play-offs, 'You can only run the four-minute mile so long.' This year Pittsburgh had to run the 'four-minute mile' to get in. This is an advantage and so is the home field. Also, their quarterback, Terry Bradshaw, is a little hurt. And on top of this, we're ready to play."

Baltimore players unanimously agreed they were approaching this play-off with a different attitude from the previous season's.

A year ago they felt lucky just to be in the play-offs. Simply being there more than accomplished their goal for the season. Beating the Steelers would have been nice, but a loss couldn't destroy their basic achievement, the magnificent comeback from 2 and 12.

George Kunz summed it up perfectly: "Last year we just felt, 'Thank God we're in the play-offs.' This year we feel, 'Now that we're here, let's go all the way.'"

The Colts also felt that having been in the play-offs would give this young team more poise and confidence the second time around.

The sellout crowd of 60,020, with not a single no-show despite local television, jammed Memorial Stadium this mild December afternoon. A dozen mounted policemen circled the field before the kickoff to discourage any fans who might wish to become personally involved in the activities thereon, the first time this had ever been deemed necessary in Baltimore.

Most experts figured this would be the best game of the entire play-offs, a mini-Super Bowl.

The Colts' game plan was to run on Pittsburgh, to try to control the pace, to wear down the Steelers' awesome defense by keeping it on the field. The Colts knew that once Pittsburgh got the ball, the Steelers also were very reluctant to give it up and the Colts were aware that their defense, especially in the secondary, was vulnerable to continued pressure.

Baltimore's hopes completely turned about between the second and third play of the game. On the second play, Pittsburgh halfback Rocky Bleier, one of the Steelers' two 1,000-yard rushers, went out for the game with a sprained big toe. But on the very next snap, the pattern of the contest was set when Terry Bradshaw collaborated with Frank Lewis on a seventy-six-yard touchdown pass. Jackie Wallace, the former Viking, was the victim.

The extra point was missed but on their next possession the Steelers used another pass from Bradshaw to Lewis to set up a forty-five-yard Roy Gerela field goal for a 9-0 lead.

The Colts fought back. As the first quarter was ending, Jones passed seventeen yards to Roger Carr for a touchdown and Toni Linhart converted to cut Pitt's lead to 9-7. The Colts were very much back in the game.

In seconds, they were out of it and for good. Theo Bell returned Linhart's kickoff sixty yards to the Baltimore thirty-two, and six running plays later the Steelers had punched over another score for 16-7. By the time the second quarter was ended they had scored seventeen points for a 26-7 half-time lead.

What had been billed as a potential classic became an actual rout. The Colts were blown out of their game plan before the intermission and lost, 40-14. "We had to play catch-up against the best catch-up defense in football," Jones said.

Bert was disconsolate, more downhearted than after any defeat Colt-watchers could remember. He steamed for long minutes in the shower before emerging to talk to reporters. "I'm going down to Louisiana and get lost for a while," he muttered.

Later he explained there was more than one reason for his anger and upset after the loss.

"If there was a year for us to go to the Super Bowl, I thought this was the year," he explained, "and so I was very upset and depressed about the ball game. When you get to the play-offs you have to win.

"Also, I don't think they used a whole lot of tact in winning. They had us beat and they still threw the ball on every down going out of the ball game. It's kind of like having somebody beat and slapping them in the face when they're down."

Marchibroda understood. He knew from personal experience how much more of himself a quarterback has to put into preparing for a big game, the hours of study at home, the extra meetings with coaches. He, too, had known the empty residue of defeat.

About all the Colts succeeded in doing was battering the Steelers to such an extent that the defending champions were eliminated in the American Conference title game by Oakland a week later. Bleier could not play against the Raiders because of his bruised toe; Franco Harris, their other 1,000-yard ground-gainer and best runner, was kayoed by the Colts with severely bruised ribs; and Roy Gerela, the kicker, missed the Oakland game because of a pulled groin muscle.

The Colts claimed no consolation from this.

The only consolation came on a different level of awareness as the Colts left the stadium and realized how close they had come to being a part of a real tragedy in Memorial Stadium and how the distasteful fact of their one-sided defeat had prevented hundreds of deaths.

During the latter stages of the game, a small private plane had been noticed buzzing the outer perimeter of the stadium.

Unknown to the huge crowd, the unstable pilot had also been buzzing Colts' workouts during the week. After a few passes safely above the light towers, he returned to the airfield and rented a new single-engine craft.

Earlier in the week he had told a friend going to the game to bring a camera. Now she would be able to use it.

Moments after the final gun, while the Steelers were celebrating in their clubhouse, the pilot, Donald Kroner, flew his two-seat Piper Cherokee in through the open end of the stadium. It looked to observers as if at first Kroner was going to try to land on the field. But at the last minute he pulled up in an attempt to fly out of the triple-decker stadium.

He didn't make it.

The sporty little plane cracked into the upper deck behind the goalposts—or home plate in the baseball configuration—and nosed over. There were no flames, no explosion. The pilot, later arrested on a variety of charges, was pulled out suffering from cuts and bruises. Three policemen suffered minor injuries.

That was all!

Because the Colts had been losing so badly, their fans had started leaving the game early. By the time Kroner pulled his little stunt, the upper deck was deserted.

If the game had been close or, God forbid, entering overtime, the section would have been jammed with spectators. Even if the Colts had been winning big, fans would have been hanging about to savor the final moments of the victory and to celebrate afterwards.

Roger Carr, the religious receiver, thought of the mysterious working of the Lord, a personal God whose intercession he credited with reversing the course of his own almost-wasted life. "It's a miracle," he thought. "Because we lost, all the people were out of the stands."

As the downhearted Colts left the stadium, still young enough to be desolated by a one-sided defeat but also young enough to be confident of their future, Baltimore firemen secured the little Piper for removal the next day.

The plane was white with blue trim, the Baltimore Colts' colors, and it somehow resembled the football team at this moment in time: wrecked, its nose out of joint, but still looking somewhat jaunty with its tail poking up at the sky as if to say, "I'll fly again."

Epilogue

The end of the 1976 campaign did not produce peace among these battling Colts. To the contrary, it signaled the renewal of open warfare.

Like a teen-ager covering her acne with makeup, the preseason truce between Ted Marchibroda and Joe Thomas had been strictly cosmetic. The sores festered, the rash spread.

Through the season, the two men barely communicated. "Oh, we spoke; but we didn't talk," is the way Marchibroda put it.

Thomas could not forgive his coach for walking out on him just before the opening game. When he learned Marchibroda wanted to take his sixteen-year-old son on one of the Colts' trips, the general manager said the boy could not travel on the team plane.

Thomas also resented the way the players had unanimously supported his rival in their summer power struggle. As the season progressed, notices began to appear with some regularity on the bulletin board eliminating various favors the club had done for the players. "Every day there was a new statement in the locker room about some minute thing they were changing, usually convenience things for us, like leaving tickets at will-call. There were a lot of rinky-dink things going on," one player complained.

As for the coaches, who generally had backed Marchibroda, Thomas didn't forget them, either. The staff, which worked long hours in dungeonlike offices below Memorial Stadium during the season, had a coffee machine there. At the end of the season Thomas sent them a bill for the coffee.

It was early November when the rumblings of discontent surfaced anew. There were rumors that Thomas wanted out. It was apparent that in the few short months since the earlier crisis owner Bob Irsay had completely reversed his position from support of Thomas to favoring Marchibroda.

Thomas still had a year to go on his contract and in early November Irsay apparently approached him about an immediate five-year renewal. At this time, the Colts were dreaming Super Bowl dreams and Thomas figured his bargaining position would be much stronger if he played out the season before committing himself.

However, Irsay blabbed about this exchange to *Chicago Tribune* sports editor Cooper Rollow. It appeared then as if Irsay was blundering into another crisis, but the way he framed this "leak," as if Thomas was looking to get out, and subsequent events indicate the club owner may have been choreographing a much larger scenario. For the first time the onus was put on Thomas as the man who wanted to change things.

Irsay told Rollow, "Marchibroda is running the team. We got all that straightened out on my yacht in Milwaukee. If there's a conflict, I'll go with Ted."

This, of course, may have come as a surprise to Marchibroda. The last thing he remembers about that conversation in Milwaukee is that he walked out of it and resigned.

Irsay also pointedly noted that if Thomas wanted to leave,

he had his replacement already on the grounds—director of pro personnel Dick Szymanski.

As the season wound down, Irsay and Thomas continued to talk. Thomas really wanted to stay. He is a man who wants to plant roots. He owned a lovely home in suburban Baltimore and there was a vacant building lot next to it. If he bought the extra lot, he could create the kind of mini-estate where a man can happily grow old. But he didn't want to make the investment without assurances that he would be around in Baltimore to enjoy it.

As best as can be reconstructed, though, Thomas set two conditions that Irsay was going to find difficult to meet. Joe wanted his new five-year contract to pay him an estimated $350,000 a year and he wanted his authority as major domo of the franchise redefined to confirm his right to fire Marchibroda.

The money was important to Thomas. He already was being paid well, but he wanted the one big contract that would provide him with final financial security.

Irsay publicly stated that Joe's salary request was out of line. "I can't afford him," the industrialist said bluntly, and he gave Thomas permission to talk to other teams. This same privilege, he noted, had not been extended to Marchibroda.

Through it all, though, Irsay kept insisting that he wanted Marchibroda and Thomas to start "acting like grown men" and reach an accommodation. Irsay did not want to break up this winning team.

If there was any hope for a reconciliation, it apparently exploded within minutes of the Colts' play-off loss to Pittsburgh.

In this postgame postmortem, Machibroda made an interesting admission. "You know, we really aren't what I would consider a Super Bowl team," he said. "We have too many weaknesses that you can get by with during the season but are exploited when you face this caliber of competition in the play-offs.

"I knew this from the beginning of the season," he added, "but of course I couldn't tell that to the players until now."

Thomas was outraged when Marchibroda's comments were relayed to him. He took them as a personal affront.

"It's the same as if I had said we had the material but we didn't get to the Super Bowl because of poor coaching," he told a friend.

Marchibroda, of course, was correct in his assessment and everybody knew it. John Dutton put his finger on the problem with some blunt talk after the loss to Pittsburgh in which Terry Bradshaw had looked like the world's greatest passer.

"A lot of quarterbacks look good against us. This is nothing new. Guys who are 35 percent throwers come in here and look like all-stars."

Dutton was referring to weaknesses in the Colts secondary that were exacerbated by a late-season injury to cornerback Nelson Munsey. An outstanding pass rush can cover up a multitude of sins in the secondary against some opponents and a high-powered offense can outscore others. But the play-offs are a different game in which balanced defense is always the key to success.

The Colts also lacked depth, which showed up in weaknesses on the special teams. Remember, the play that really beat Baltimore was Theo Bell's sixty-yard kickoff return.

Everybody knew all this, including most certainly Joe Thomas. He just didn't want to be publicly reminded.

The situation came to a head in the weeks surrounding the Super Bowl.

Thomas, exploring other avenues after being given leave by Irsay, came very close to hooking on with Atlanta. The Falcons needed a strong leader and were willing to give Joe all the authority he needed.

The deal seemed set, then collapsed.

According to one source, it may have foundered when Falcons owner Rankin Smith asked Thomas for a definition of "total control."

Joe reportedly answered, "That means you get on a boat when the season starts and come back after it's over and say, 'How did we do?' "

Smith and his associates had paid $8.5 million for the expansion team in 1965. They wanted more for their money than that.

The Monday before the Super Bowl, Marchibroda met with Irsay in Chicago to spell out some of the conditions he would require to remain as coach. Again he asked for no responsibility for the college draft, merely that he wanted control over his personnel and staff.

The next day, Irsay pulled another of his bizarre stunts by calling Bert Jones to ask the quarterback to intervene with Thomas, to ask Thomas to accept Marchibroda's conditions.

Aware that he was being sucked into dangerous waters, Bert brought his father along with him to the meeting with Irsay.

That Friday, on the eve of the Super Bowl, Bert was in Los Angeles to receive the Schick-Pro Football Writers of America award as most valuable player in the NFL. He called Thomas at his hotel to try to arrange a meeting.

Thomas reacted belligerently.

"Who do you think you are to advise me?" he reportedly demanded of the quarterback. "You think you're the best quarterback in football, well I think I'm the best general manager."

Thomas refused to meet with Jones personally and the quarterback was shaken by the snub.

"I sent a boy into the lion's den," said Irsay, conceding his mistake, "but I had to try every possible way to keep both men."

The next Friday, Marchibroda met with Thomas in Baltimore at Irsay's request in one last attempt to resolve their differences.

But instead of seeking a reconciliation, Thomas went on the offensive. "Do you want permission to go elsewhere?" he demanded.

Afterward Thomas put it bluntly on a him-or-me basis with Irsay and told his owner he had given Marchibroda permission to look for another job. At this point, Thomas was finished with the Colts. Irsay reminded Thomas that he had exceeded his authority by telling Marchibroda he could look elsewhere. And he told intimates that the general manager would be fired within the week.

Over the weekend, Thomas and Irsay were together, representing the Colts at the league meetings held in Seattle to coincide with the Pro Bowl. They sat next to each other during the formal meetings, but barely spoke. Thomas looked like a shaken, beaten man. Like a seasoned boxer, Irsay had spun out of the corner he'd found himself in back in September and now Thomas was pinned against the ropes.

For perhaps the first time in his life Thomas ducked questions by saying, "My lawyers have told me to keep my mouth shut." He pointed out that he was still being paid by the Colts but he also lost his cool and publicly berated the reporter (Cameron Snyder of the *Baltimore Sun*) who had broken the story of his imminent ouster as general manager.

Short days after the Pro Bowl Irsay's attorneys delivered notice to Thomas that he had been fired. He predictably declined their offer to let it be announced that he had "resigned." There still were problems over the last year of his contract and the question of payment was given over to Commissioner Pete Rozelle to settle.

Irsay made no secret of the reason for his mid-season switch from Thomas to Marchibroda. "Why is Ted here and Joe gone?" Irsay asked the *News-American*'s John Steadman. "Because the people of Baltimore and the players wanted Ted here and Joe told me he couldn't live with Ted and so there was no choice. If Ted goes, then the coaches and Bert Jones go, too, and I won't let that happen."

Once again, Bert Jones, The Franchise, had been the decisive consideration.

Thomas's departure brought about a thorough shake-up in the Colts' front office. Marchibroda was offered the general manager's title and declined it, content with his new position as strong man on the club with total control of the football operation, including draft and trades.

Szymanski, a loyal Colt since they drafted him as a player out of Notre Dame in 1955, was promoted to general manager. He would direct the business side of the operation. Ernie Accorsi returned from the league office to become assistant GM.

As for Joe Thomas, he may have been counted out in Baltimore, but he didn't stay on the canvas very long. Within two months he had found a new angel, the San Francisco Forty-niners were for sale and Joe was back in business with a franchise to run. Maybe in the shadow of the Golden Gate he could find his home and that even more elusive "total control," and just to make sure he promptly unloaded the popular incumbent coach, Monte Clark. Soon after, Marty Domres followed his coach out of town on waivers.

Marchibroda, in one of his first acts, let go two assistants he had inherited from previous regimes, end coach Pete McCulley and Jerry Smith, who was in charge of the defensive line. Marchibroda undoubtedly considered them "Thomas men" and wanted to be surrounded by his own people.

One of the first problems facing Szymanski in a sense had been instigated by Thomas. John Dutton, Roger Carr, and George Kunz, three of the Colts' Pro Bowl players, were all represented by the same agent, Howard Slusher of Los Angeles, and all three would be entering their option seasons in 1977. They served notice that they planned to act in concert to get the best new deal possible, though each would negotiate separately. They said the published salary demands of Joe Thomas had spurred them to seek big money themselves. "He doesn't even put on a uniform, but if he's worth that much, so are we," Carr explained, and the others concurred.

However, no matter what problems or defections he faced, Marchibroda knew he still had The Franchise on his side. In Bert Jones, Marchibroda and the Colts had a young man acknowledged as the premier quarterback in pro football.

"He is in a class by himself," summed up a pretty fair quarterback whom Jones himself ranks as the greatest "pure passer that ever lived"—Joe Namath.

During the '76 season, Bert had completed more than 60 percent of his passes for twenty-four touchdowns with only nine interceptions. One of these interceptions, which bounced out of the intended receiver's hands in the last game of the season, was all that cost him the NFL passing championship.

Ted Marchibroda was sitting in the big corner office in the Colts' plush offices high in a modern suburban high-rise office complex. Sun streamed in through huge windows that gave the room two exposures.

He talked about his quarterback.

"People asked me how great Bert Jones can be and I say when you've had the kind of statistics he has had for the last two years, you just hope that he maintains them. That's all we ask, that he maintain this level of performance.

"The big change in Bert came between the 1975 and '76 season," Marchibroda continued. "In '75 he tried to do it all just with his arm. But the next season he developed an awareness of how he could use all his other weapons, like the running game.

"The most amazing factor of all this, though, is that it had taken place so quickly, in only two years. He picked up everything much quicker than I expected. You could say he has played beyond his experience."

There were also intangible satisfactions for Marchibroda. "It's a great thing in your life when you put your faith in a quarterback and they respond," he said and he noted he had helped create this without tampering with Bert's native ability or technique. "He's got a style of his own," Marchibroda said, "just like when you saw Unitas drop back, you knew it was Unitas."

All through the off-season, accolades poured in for Bert. He was almost everybody's Most Valuable Player. Except for one week penciled in to go over the old season and plan for the new with Marchibroda, he spent the off-season accepting awards, tending to his various business interests, and marrying the beautiful Danni. Occasionally he pondered his football future.

As a ball boy, Bert had been with the Cleveland Browns when they helped dedicate the new Pro Football Hall of Fame in Canton, Ohio, in 1963. He remembers touring the building and being impressed, but the main desire of this teen-ager, naturally, was to see the game that was scheduled for that afternoon.

He doesn't think of himself yet in Hall of Fame terms. It is much too soon.

But it is not too soon to think of goals.

"My goal is to be the best," he says. "I feel I can be the best and I feel I will be the best and that's what I am striving for."

And how will he know that he has arrived at this level, if ever?

"By winning," he answered. "That's where the worth of a quarterback shows up."

Records Section

Bert Jones at LSU

VARSITY STATISTICS

Year	Passing						Total Offense			TD
	Att.	Comp.	Pct.	HI	Yds.	TD	Rush	Pass	Total	Resblty.
1970	100	52	.520	5	864	5	-64	864	800	5
1971	119	65	.546	4	945	9	- 7	945	938	13
1972	199	103	.518	7	1446	14	18	1446	1464	18
TOTALS	418	220	.526	16	3255	28	-53	3255	3202	36

SCHOOL RECORDS

CAREER

Most Plays, Total Offense	631
Most Yards, Total Offense	3,202
Most Touchdowns Responsible For	36
Most Passes Attempted	418
Most Passes Completed	220
Most Yardage Passing	3,255
Most Touchdown Passes	28
Lowest Interception Percentage	.038
(16 of 418 att.)	
Highest Percentage Passes Completed	
(minimum 400 att.)	.526

SEASON

Most Plays, Total Offense	289
Most Yards, Total Offense	1,464
Most Touchdowns Responsible For	18
Most Passes Attempted	199
Most Passes Completed	103
Most Yardage Passing	1,446
Most Yards Gained Per Game	133.1
Most Touchdown Passes	14

GAME

Most Passes Completed	18 (vs. Alabama, 11-11-72)
Most Yards Passing	242 (vs. Alabama, 11-11-72)
Highest Average Gain Per Play	10.9 (vs. Auburn, 10-14-72)

(*Note*: Tied record for most touchdown passes in one game, 3)

(vs. Tulane, 11-27-71)
(vs. Texas A & M, 9-23-72)
(vs. Auburn, 10-14-72)

Only LSU player to have accomplished this more than once.

Bert Jones as a Colt

REGULAR SEASON

PASSING	G	Att-Cmp	Yards	Pcts.	Int.	LG	TD
1973	8	108-43	539	39.8	12	51	4
1974	11	270-143	1610	53.0	12	57	8
1975	14	344-203	2483	59.0	8	90t	18
1976	14	343-207	3104	60.4	9	79t	24
Career	47	1065-596	7736	55.7	41	90t	54

RUSHING			No.	Yards	Avg.	LG	TD
1973			18	58	3.2	17	0
1974			39	279	7.2	39	4
1975			47	321	6.8	36	3
1976			38	214	5.6	17	2
Career			142	872	6.1	39	9

POSTSEASON

PASSING	Att-Cmp	Yards	Pct.	Int.	LG	TD
1975 at Pittsburgh	11-6	91	54.5	0	58	0
1976 at Pittsburgh	25-11	144	44.0	2	25	1
Career	36-17	235	47.2	2	58	1

RUSHING	No.	Yards	Avg.	LG	TD
1975 at Pittsburgh	2	6	3.0	7	0
1976 at Pittsburgh	2	3	1.5	3	0
Career	4	9	2.3	7	0

GAME-BY-GAME PASSING

1973	Att-Cmp	Yards	Int.	LG	TD
at Cleveland	22-6	56	1	33t	1
N.Y. Jets*	23-12	176	4	51	1
New Orleans*	16-7	91	4	33	1
at New England*	19-8	109	0	48	1
at Buffalo*	15-7	71	2	17	0
at Detroit	DNP				
Oakland	2-0	0	0	0	0
Houston	DNP				
at Miami	11-3	36	1	37	0
at Washington	0-0	0	0	0	0

Buffalo, at N.Y. Jets, Miami, New England—DNP.

1974	Att-Cmp	Yards	Int.	LG	TD
at Pittsburgh	17-8	100	2	27	0
Green Bay	16-7	88	1	19	1
at Philadelphia	22-12	141	1	24	1
at New England*	41-22	215	1	45	0
Buffalo*	16-6	44	1	12	0
at N.Y. Jets*	17-11	106	0	17	1
at Miami*	17-7	73	0	28	0
Cincinnati*	18-9	108	1	31	0
Denver, at Atlanta, New England—DNP, shoulder separation.					
at Buffalo*	27-11	170	1	45	0
Miami*	26-14	180	0	57	1
N.Y. Jets*	53-36	385	4	39	4

1975	Att-Cmp	Yards	Int.	LG	TD
at Chicago*	24-15	177	0	22	2
Oakland*	43-21	307	1	49	1
at Los Angeles	25-14	155	2	29	2
Buffalo*	23-11	155	1	54	2
at New England*	24-12	70	0	14	0
at N.Y. Jets*	25-17	209	0	68t	2
Cleveland*	26-16	153	1	35t	2
at Buffalo*	22-14	306	1	89t	2
N.Y. Jets*	22-16	277	1	90t	3
at Miami*	10-4	26	0	8	0
Kansas City*	13-12	145	0	58	1
at N.Y. Giants*	17-10	90	0	28	0
Miami*	39-23	232	0	17	0
New England*	31-18	181	1	20t	1
at Pittsburgh (AFC Playoff)	11-6	91	0	58	0

1976	Att-Cmp	Yards	Int.	LG	TD
at New England*	23-17	190	0	25	2
Cincinnati*	29-14	301	3	68	3
at Dallas*	31-13	237	0	49	0
Tampa Bay*	24-15	186	0	48	2
Miami*	14-11	177	0	48	1
at Buffalo*	33-13	207	0	39	2
at N.Y. Jets*	27-16	297	1	79t	2
Houston*	28-19	197	0	39	0
at San Diego*	25-18	275	1	41	3
New England*	25-10	139	2	55	1
at Miami*	20-13	234	0	54	1
N.Y. Jets*	32-22	175	0	31	3
at St. Louis*	23-13	241	1	30	1
Buffalo*	20-13	248	1	47	3
Pittsburgh (AFC Playoff)*	25-11	235	2	25	1

*Games started

CAREER HIGHS

Most attempts—53 vs. N.Y. Jets, Dec. 15, 1974; **Most completions**—36 vs. N.Y. Jets, Dec. 15, 1974; **Most Yardage**—385 vs. N.Y. Jets, Dec. 15, 1974; **Most touchdowns**—4 vs. N.Y. Jets, Dec. 15, 1974; **Long**—90t vs. N.Y. Jets, Nov. 16, 1975; **Most interceptions**—4 vs. N.Y. Jets, Sept. 23, 1973, vs. New Orleans, Sept. 30, 1973, vs. N.Y. Jets, Dec. 15, 1974.

Bert Jones Awards

COLLEGIATE

Consensus All-America at LSU
Selected Player of the Year by the *Sporting News* and Cleveland Touchdown Club
Named M.V.P. at LSU his senior year

PROFESSIONAL

1975: Colt Most Valuable Player (selected by teammates for NEA)
Honorable Mention U.P.I. AFC All-Star Team
1976: 1976 All-NFL Team (AP, NEA, PFWA)
1976 Associated Press All-Pro Team (first team)
1976 NEA All-Pro Team (first team)
1976 PFWA All-Pro Team (first team)
All-AFC Team (AP, UPI)
Seagram's Seven Crowns of Sports Award: M.V.P.
Kansas City's 101 Award: AFC Offensive Player of the Year
NFLPA M.V.P. Award
Schick-Pro Football Writers of America M.V.P. Award
AP M.V.P. Award
New York Daily News M.V.P. Award

All-Pro Colts
First-team selections only

1953—Tom Keane, HB
1954—Art Donovan, DT
1955—Alan Ameche, FB; Art Donovan, DT; Bert Rechichar, HB
1956—Art Donovan, DT; Gino Marchetti, DE
1957—Milt Davis, DHB; Art Donovan, DT; Gino Marchetti, DE; John Unitas, QB
1958—Raymond Berry, WR; Gene Lipscomb, DT; Gino Marchetti, DE; Lenny Moore, RB; Jim Parker, T; John Unitas, QB
1959—Raymond Berry, WR; Gene Lipscomb, DT; Gino Marchetti, DE; Lenny Moore, RB; Andy Nelson, DHB; Jim Parker, T; Art Spinney, G; John Unitas, QB
1960—Raymond Berry, WR; Gene Lipscomb, DT; Gino Marchetti, DE; Lenny Moore, RB; Jim Parker, T
1961—Gino Marchetti, DE; Lenny Moore, RB; Jim Parker, T
1962—Gino Marchetti, DE; Jim Parker, G-T
1963—Gino Marchetti, DE; Jim Parker, G
1964—Bob Boyd, DHB; Gino Marchetti, DE; Lenny Moore, RB; Jim Parker, G; John Unitas, QB; Bob Vogel, T
1965—Bob Boyd, DHB; Jimmy Orr, Fl; Jim Parker, G; John Unitas, QB; Bob Vogel, T
1966—Bob Boyd, DHB; John Mackey, TE
1967—John Mackey, TE; Willie Richardson, Fl; John Unitas, QB; Bob Vogel, T
1968—Bob Boyd, DHB; Mike Curtis, LB; John Mackey, TE; Earl Morrall, QB; Bob Vogel, T; Rick Volk, S
1969—David Lee, P
1970—David Lee, P; Jerry Logan, S; Bubba Smith, DE; Rick Volk, S
1971—Ted Hendricks, LB; Bubba Smith, DE; Rick Volk, S
1975—George Kunz, T
1976—John Dutton, DE; Bert Jones, QB

All-Time Colt Roster

The following compilation of Colt alumni includes every player who has been on the active roster for at least three games in any single season since 1953.

COACHES

Arnsparger, Bill—Miami (O.)	1964-69	McCulley, Pete—Louisiana Tech	1973-76
Ball, Herman—Davis-Elkins	1956-62	Miller, Red—Western Illinois	1971-72
Baughan, Maxie—Georgia Tech	1975-76	Moiesworth, Keith—Monmouth	1953
Bielski, Dick—Maryland	1964-72	Murphy, Russ—Davidson	1954
Boutselis, George—N. Carolina	1975-76	Mutscheller, Jim—Notre Dame	1963
Boyd, Bob—Oklahoma	1969-72	Noll, Chuck—Dayton	1966-67
Bridgers, John—Auburn	1957-58	Pellington, Bill—Rutgers	1963
Bullough, Hank—Michigan State	1970-72	Richards, Ray—Nebraska	1953
Callahan, Ray—Kentucky	1973	Rymkus, Lou—Notre Dame	1970
Cumiskey, Frank—Ohio State	1954-56	Sandusky, John—Villanova	1959-72
Doll, Don—USC	1974	Schnellenberger, Howard—	
Douglas, Otis—Wm. & Mary	1953	Kentucky	1973-74
Dovell, Whitey—Maryland	1975-76	Setcik, George—Notre Dame	1973
Ewbank, Weeb—Miami (O.)	1954-62	Shaw, Bob—Ohio State	1957-58
Franklin, Bobby—Mississippi	1973	Shula, Don—John Carroll	1963-69
Hughes, Tom—Purdue	1955	Smith, Jerry—Wisconsin	1974-76
Idzik, John—Maryland	1970-72	Szymanski, Dick—Notre Dame	1974
Lauterbur, Frank—		Thomas, Joe—Ohio Northern	1954, 74
Mt. Union	1955-56, 74-76	Voris, Dick—San Jose State	1973
Marchetti, Gino—USF	1963	Wasylik, Nick—Ohio State	1953
Marchibroda, Ted—		Winner, Charlie—Washington	1954-65
St. Bonaventure	1975-76	Young, George—Bucknell	1970, 73
McCafferty, Don—Ohio State	1960-72		

PLAYERS

Agase, Alex (G) Illinois	1953	Bighead, Jack (E) Pepperdine	1954
Allen, Gerald (B) Omaha	1966	Blandin, Ernie (T) Tulane	1953
Alley, Don (F) Adams State	1967	Blue, Forrest (C) Auburn	1975-76
Ameche, Alan (B) Wisconsin	1955-60	Bieick, Tom (B) Georgia	1956
Amman, Richard (DE)		Boyd, Bob (DB) Oklahoma	1960-68
Florida State	1972-73	Braase, Ordell (DE) S. Dakota	1957-68
Andrews, John (TE) Indiana	1973-74	Brethauer, Monte (E) Oregon	1953, 55
Austin, Ocie (DB) Utah State	1968-69	Brown, Barry (E) Florida	1966-67
Averno, Sisto (G) Muhlenberg	1953-54	Brown, Ed (QB) USF	1965
Bailey, Jim (DT) Kansas	1970-74	Brown, Ray (DB) Mississippi	1958-60
Baldwin, Bob (B) Clemson	1966-67	Brown, Timmy (RB) Ball State	1968
Ball, Sam (T) Kentucky	1966-70	Bryan, Walter (B) Texas Tech	1955
Barnes, Mike (DE) Miami (Fla.)	1973-76	Burkett, Jack (LB) Auburn	1961-66
Barwegen, Dick (G) Purdue	1953-54	Bulaich, Norm (RB) TCU	1970-72
Baylor, Tim (DB) Morgan State	1976	Call, Jack (B) Colgate	1957-58
Berra, Tim (WR) Massachusetts	1974	Campanella, Joe (T) Ohio State	1953-57
Berry, Raymond (E) SMU	1955-67	Campbell, John (LB) Minnesota	1969
Bertuca, Tony (LB) Chico State	1974	Carr, Roger (WR) Louisiana Tech	1974-76
Beutler, Tom (LB) Toledo	1971	Cheatham, Ernie (T) Loyola LA	1954
Bielski, Dick (E) Maryland	1962-63	Cherry, Stan (LB) Morgan State	1973

Chester, Raymond (TE)
Morgan State 1973-76
Cheyunski, Jim (LB) Syracuse 1975-76
Chrovich, Dick (T) Miami (O.) 1955-56
Clemens, Bob (B) Pitt 1962
Cogdill, Gail (E) Washington State 1968
Cole, Terry (RB) Indiana 1968-69
Collett, Elmer (G) SF State 1973-76
Colteryahn, Lloyd (E) Maryland 1954-56
Colvin, Jim (T) Houston 1960-63
Conjar, Larry (B) Notre Dame 1969-70
Cook, Fred (DE) So. Mississippi 1974-76
Cooke, Ed (E) Maryland 1959
Coutre, Larry (B) Notre Dame 1953
Craddock, Nate (RB) Parsons 1963
Cuozzo, Gary (QB) Virginia 1963-66
Curry, Bill (C) Georgia Tech 1967-72
Curtis, Mike (LB) Duke 1965-75
Curtis, Tom (DB) Michigan 1970-71
Davidson, Cotton (QB) Baylor 1954, 57
Davis, Milt (DB) UCLA 1957-60
Davis, Norman (G) Grambling 1967
Davis, Ted (LB) Georgia Tech 1964-66
DeCarlo, Art (E) Georgia 1957-60
DelBello, Jack (B) Miami (Fla.) 1953
Dickel, Dan (LB) Iowa 1974-76
Diehl, John (T) Virginia 1961-64
Domres, Marty (QB) Columbia 1972-75
Donovan, Art (DT) Boston Coll. 1953-61
Doughty, Glenn (WR) Michigan 1972-76
Drougas, Tom (T) Oregon 1972-73
Duncan, James (DB) Md. State 1969-71
Dunlap, Len (DB) N. Tex. State 1971
Dunn, Perry Lee (RB) Mississippi 1969
Dupre, L. G. (RB) Baylor 1955-59
Dutton, John (DE) Nebraska 1974-76
Ecklund, Brad (C) Oregon 1953
Edmunds, Randy (LB)
Georgia Tech 1972
Edwards, Dan (E) Georgia 1953-54
Eggers, Doug (LB)
S. Dakota State 1954-57
Ehrmann, Joe (DT) Syracuse 1973-76
Embree, Mel (E) Pepperdine 1953
Enke, Fred (QB) Arizona 1953-54
Feagin, Wiley (G) Houston 1961-62
Feamster, Tom (T) Florida State 1956
Felts, Bob (B) Florida A&M 1965
Fernandes, Ron (DE)
Eastern Michigan 1976
Finnin, Tom (DT) Detroit 1953-56
Flowers, Bernie (E) Purdue 1956
Flowers, Dick (B) Northwestern 1953
Franklin, Willie (WR) Oklahoma 1972

Ganas, Rusty (DT) S. Carolina 1971
Gardin, Ron (DB) Arizona 1970
Gaubatz, Dennis (LB) LSU 1965-69
George, Ed (T) Wake Forest 1975
Gilburg, Tom (T) Syracuse 1961-65
Ginn, Hubert (RB) Florida A&M 1973
Glick, Gary (B) Colo. A&M 1961
Goode, Tom (C) Mississippi State 1970
Grant, Bob (LB) Wake Forest 1968-70
Gregory, Ken (E) Whittier 1961
Grimm, Dan (G) Colorado 1969
Hall, Randy (CB) Idaho 1974, 76
Harness, Jim (B) Mississippi State 1956
Harold, George (B) Allen 1966-67
Harris, Wendell (DB) LSU 1962-65
Harrison, Bob (B) Ohio U. 1961
Havrilak, Sam (B) Bucknell 1969-73
Hawkins, Alex (B)
South Carolina 1955-65, 67-68
Haymond, Alvin (DB)
Southern U. 1964-67
Hendricks, Ted (LB) Miami (Fla.) 1969-73
Hepburn, Lonnie (CB) Texas So. 1971-72
Hermann, John (B) UCLA 1956
Herosian, Brian (S) Connecticut 1973
Hill, Jerry (RB) Wyoming 1961, 63-70
Hilton, Roy (DE) Jackson State 1965-73
Hinton, Chuck (DT) N. Carolina Col. 1972
Hinton, Ed (WR) Oklahoma 1969-72
Hoaglin, Fred (C) Pitt. 1973
Horn, Dick (B) Stanford 1958
Huff, Ken (G) N. Carolina 1975-76
Hugasian, Harry (B) Stanford 1955
Hunt, George (K) Tennessee 1973
Huzvar, John (RB) Pitt. 1953-54
Jackson, Ken (G) Texas 1953-57
James, Tommy (B) Ohio State 1956
Jefferson, Roy (WR) Utah 1970
Johnson, Cornelius (G)
Va. Union 1968-72
Johnson, Marshall (WR) Houston 1975
Jones, Bert (QB) LSU 1973-76
Joyce, Don (DE) Tulane 1954-60
Kaczmarek, Mike (LB) Southern Ill. 1973
Kalmanir, Tom (B) Nevada 1953
Keane, Tom (DB) W. Virginia 1953-54
Kennedy, Jimmie (TE)
Colorado State 1975-76
Kerkorian, Gary (QB)
Stanford 1954-56, 58
Kern, Rex (DB) Ohio State 1971-73
Kirchiro, Bill (G) Maryland 1962
Kirkland, Mike (QB) Arkansas 1976
Kirouac, Lou (T) Boston Coll. 1964

Koman, Bill (G) North Carolina 1956
Kostelnik, Ron (T) Cincinnati 1969
Kovac, Ed (B) Cincinnati 1960
Krouse, Ray (DE) Maryland 1958
Kunz, George (T) Notre Dame 1975-76
Laird, Bruce (DB)
  American International 1972-76
Langas, Bob (E) Wayne 1954
Lange, Bill (G) Dayton 1953
Larson, Lynn (T) Kansas State 1971-72
Laskey, Bill (LB) Michigan 1971-72
Leaks, Roosevelt (RB) Texas 1975-76
Leberman, Bob (B) Syracuse 1954
Lee, David (P) Louisiana Tech 1966-76
Lee,. Monte (C) Texas 1965
Lee, Ron (RB) West Virginia 1976
Lesane, Jimmy (B) Virginia 1954
Lewis, Harold (B) Houston 1959
Lewis, Joe (T) Compton 1961
Linhart, Toni (K) Austria Tech 1974-76
Linne, Aubrey (E) TCU 1961
Lipscomb, Gene (DT) Miller H.S. 1956-60
Little, Jack (T) Texas A&M 1953-54
Lockett, J.W. (B) Okla. Central 1963
Logan, Jerry (DB)
  W. Texas State 1963-72
Looney, Joe Don (RB) Oklahoma 1964
Lorick, Tony (RB) Arizona State 1964-67
Luce, Derrel (LB) Baylor 1975-76
Lyles, Lenny (DB) Louisville 1958, 61-69
Mackey, Dee (E)
  E. Texas State 1961-62
Mackey, John (TE) Syracuse 1963-72
MacLeod, Tom (LB) Minnesota 1974-75
Maitland, Jack (RB) Williams 1970
Maples, Butch (C) Baylor 1963
Marchetti, Gino (DE) USF 1953-64, 66
Martin, Jim (K) Notre Dame 1963
Matte, Tom (RB) Ohio State 1961-72
Matusak, Marv (B) Tulsa 1959-61
Mauck, Carl (LB) So. Illinois 1969
Maxwell, Tom (B) Texas A&M 1969-70
May, Ray (LB) USC 1970-72
Mayo, Ron (TE) Morgan State 1974
McCauley, Don (RB) N. Carolina 1971-76
McHan, Lamar (QB) Arkansas 1961-63
McMillan, Chuck (B) John Carroll 1954
McPhail, Buck (RB) Oklahoma 1953
Memmelaar, Dale (G) Wyoming 1966-67
Mendenhall, Ken (C) Oklahoma 1971-76
Michaels, Lou (DE, K) Kentucky 1964-69
Mildren, Jack (S) Oklahoma 1972-73
Miller, Fred (DT) LSU 1963-72
Mioduszewski, Ed (B) Wm. & Mary 1953
Mitchell, Lydell (RB) Penn State 1972-76

Mitchell, Tom (TE) Bucknell 1968-73
Mooney, Ed (LB) Texas Tech 1972-73
Moore, Henry (B) Arkansas 1957
Moore, Lenny (RB) Penn State 1956-67
Morrall, Earl (QB)
  Michigan State 1968-71
Mosier, John (TE) Kansas 1972
Moss, Roland (RB, TE) Toledo 1969
Mumphord, Lloyd (CB)
  Texas So. 1975-76
Munsey, Nelson (CB) Wyoming 1972-76
Mutscheller, Jim (E) Notre Dame 1954-61
Myers, Bob (T) Ohio State 1955
Myhra, Steve (LB, K) N. Dakota 1957-61
Neal, Dan (C) Kentucky 1973-74
Nelson, Andy (DB)
  Memphis State 1957-63
Nelson, Dennis (T) Illinois State 1970-74
Nettles, Doug (CB) Vanderbilt 1974-75
Newsome, Billy (DE) Grambling 1970-72
Nichols, Robbie (LB) Tulsa 1970-71
Nottingham, Don (RB)
  Kent State 1971-73
Novak, Ken (DT) Purdue 1976
Nowatzke, Tom (RB) Indiana 1970-72
Nutter, Buzz (C) VPI 1954-60, 65
Nyers, Dick (B) Indiana Central 1956-57
O'Brien, Jim (K, WR) Cincinnati 1970-72
Oldham, Ray (S)
  Middle Tennessee State 1973-76
Olds, Bill (RB) Nebraska 1973-75
Orduna, Joe (RB) Nebraska 1974
Orr, Jimmy (E) Georgia 1961-70
Owens, Luke (T) Kent State 1957
Owens, R.C. (E) Coll. of Idaho 1962
Parker, Jim (T, G) Ohio State 1957-67
Patera, Jack (LB) Oregon 1955-57
Pear, Dave (DT) Washington 1975
Pearson, Preston (RB) Illinois 1967-68
Pellington, Bill (LB) Rutgers 1953-64
Pepper, Gene (G) Mississippi 1954
Perkins, Ray (WR) Alabama 1967-71
Perry, Joe (RB) Compton 1961-62
Peterson, Gerald (T) Texas 1956
Petties, Neal (E)
  San Diego State 1964-66
Pittman, Charlie (RB) Penn State 1971
Plunkett, Sherm (T) Md. State 1958-60
Poole, Barney (E) Army, Mississippi 1953
Porter, Ron (LB) Idaho 1967-69
Pratt, Robert (G) N. Carolina 1974-76
Preas, George (T) VPI 1955-65
Pricer, Billy (RB) Oklahoma 1957-60
Pyle, Palmer (G) Michigan St. 1960-63
Radosevich, George (C) Pitt. 1954-56

Raiff, Jim (G) Dayton	1954	Speyrer, Cotton (WR) Texas	1972-74
Rechichar, Bert (DB, K) Tenn.	1953-59	Spinney, Art (G) Boston Coll.	1953-60
Reese, Guy (T) SMU	1964-65	Stevens, Howard (RB) Louisville	1975-76
Renfro, Dean (B) N. Texas State	1955	Stone, Avatus (B) Syracuse	1958
Ressler, Glenn (G) Penn State	1965-74	Stonebreaker, Steve (LB) Detroit	1964-66
Rhodes, Danny (LB) Arkansas	1974	Strofolino, Mike (LB) Villanova	1965
Richardson, Jerry (E) Wolford	1959-60	Stukes, Charles (DB) Md. State	1967-72
Richardson, Willie (WR)		Stynchula, Andy (T) Penn State	1966-67
Jackson State	1963-69, 71	Sullivan, Dan (G, T)	
Riley, Butch (LB) Texas A&I	1969	Boston College	1962-72
Robinson, Chas. (G) Morgan State	1954	Szymanski, Dick (C, LB)	
Robinson, Glenn (DE)		Notre Dame	1955, 57-68
Oklahoma State	1975	Taliaferro, George (B) Indiana	1953-54
Rudnick, Tim (DB) Notre Dame	1974	Taseff, Carl (B) John Carroll	1953-61
Salter, Bryant (DB) Pittsburgh	1976	Taylor, David (T) Catawba	1973-76
Sample, John (DB)		Thomas, Jesse (B)	
Maryland State	1958-60	Michigan State	1955-57
Sandusky, Alex (G) Clarion	1954-66	Thompson, Don (DE) Richmond	1962-63
Sanford, Leo (C) Louisiana Tech	1958	Thompson, Ricky (WR) Baylor	1976
Saul, Bill (LB) Penn State	1962-63	Thurston, Fred (G) Valparaiso	1958
Schmiesing, Joe (DT-DE)		Toth, Zollie (RB) LSU	1953-54
New Mexico State	1973	Troup, Bill (QB) S. Carolina	1974, 76
Scott, Freddie (WR) Amherst	1974-76	Turner, Bake (E) Texas Tech	1962
Sharkey, Ed (G) Duke, Nevada	1953	Unitas, John (QB) Louisville	1956-72
Shaw, George (QB) Oregon	1955-58	Van Duyne, Bob (G) Idaho	1974-76
Sherer, Dave (E) SMU	1959	Varty, Mike (LB) Northwestern	1975
Shields, Burrell (B) John Carroll	1955	Vessels, Billy (RB) Oklahoma	1956
Shields, Lebron (G) Tennessee	1960	Vogel, Bob (T) Ohio State	1963-72
Shinners, John (G) Xavier	1972	Volk, Rick (DB) Michigan	1967-75
Shinnick, Don (LB) UCLA	1957-68	Wallace, Jackie (S) Arizona	1975-76
Shiver, Sanders (LB)		Ward, Jim (QB) Gettysburg	1967-69
Carson-Newman	1976	Welch, Jim (B) SMU	1960-67
Shlapak, Boris (K) Michigan St.	1972	White, Bob (B) Stanford	1955
Shula, Don (DB) John Carroll	1953-56	White, Stan (LB) Ohio State	1972-76
Simonini, Ed (LB) Texas A&M	1976	Williams, John (G) Minnesota	1968-72
Simonson, Dave (T) Minnesota	1974	Williams, Steve (DT) Western Car.	1974
Simpson, Jack (B) Florida	1958-60	Wilson, Butch (E) Alabama	1963-67
Smith, Billy Ray (T) Arkansas	1961-70	Windauer, Bill (DT) Iowa	1973-74
Smith, Bubba (DE)		Wingate, Elmer (E) Maryland	1953
Michigan State	1967-71	Winkler, Jim (T) Texas A&M	1953
Smith, Ollie (WR)		Womble, Royce (RB)	
Tennessee State	1973-74	N. Texas State	1954-57
Smith, Zeke (LB) Auburn	1960	Wright, George (DT) Houston	1970-71
Smolinski, Mark (B) Wyoming	1961-62	Yohn, Dave (C) Gettysburg	1962
Sommers, Mike (RB)		Young, Buddy (B) Illinois	1953-55
Geo. Washington	1959-61	Young, Dick (B) Chattanooga	1955-56

Colts' Biggest Games

NFL CHAMPIONSHIP
Dec. 28, 1958 Yankee Stadium

Baltimore 23, New York 17

Baltimore	0	14	0	3	6—23
New York	3	0	7	7	0—17

NY—FG Summerall 36
Balt—Ameche 2 plunge (Myhra kick)
Balt—Berry 15 pass from Unitas (Myhra kick)
NY—Triplett 1 plunge (Summerall kick)
NY—Gifford 15 pass from Conerly (Summerall kick)
Balt—FG Myhra 20
Balt—Ameche 1 plunge (No conversion attempted)

Stat Leaders

Passing
Balt—Unitas (26-40-349), 1 TD, 1 Int, L-60
NY—Conerly (10-14-187), 1 TD, 0 Int, L-67, Heinrich (2-4-13)

Rushing
Balt—Ameche (14-65), Dupre (11-30), Moore (8-23), Unitas (6-20)
NY—Gifford (12-60), Webster (12-24)

Receiving
Balt—Berry (12-178), Moore (6-101), Mutscheller (3-46)
NY—Rote (2-76), Schnelker (2-63)
ATT: 64,185.

NFL CHAMPIONSHIP
Dec. 27, 1959 Baltimore Memorial Stadium

Baltimore 31, New York 16

New York	3	3	3	7—16
Baltimore	7	0	0	24—31

Balt—Moore 59 pass from Unitas (Myhra kick)
NY—FG Summerall 23
NY—FG Summerall 37
NY—FG Summerall 22
Balt—Unitas 4 run (Myhra kick)
Balt—Richardson 12 pass from Unitas (Myhra kick)
Balt—Sample 42 intercepted pass (Myhra kick)
Balt—FG Myhra 25
NY—Schnelker 32 pass from Conerly (Summerall kick)

Stat Leaders

Passing
Balt—Unitas (18-29-264), 2 TDs, 0 Int, L-59
NY—Conerly (16-35-232), 0 TDs, 2 Int, L-48

Rushing
Balt—Ameche (9-31), Sommer (6-15), Pricer (4-14), Moore (4-7)
NY—Gifford (9-50), Triplett (5-37), Webster (8-25)

Receiving
Balt—Moore (3-126), Berry (5-68), Mutscheller (5-40)
NY—Schnelker (9-175), Rote (2-41), King (4-17), Gifford (1-19)
ATT: 57,545.

NFL CHAMPIONSHIP
Dec. 27, 1964 Cleveland Stadium

Cleveland 27, Baltimore 0

Baltimore	0	0	0	0— 0
Cleveland	0	0	17	10—27

Cleve—FG Groza 43
Cleve—Collins 18 pass from Ryan (Groza kick)
Cleve—Collins 42 pass from Ryan (Groza kick)
Cleve—Collins 51 pass from Ryan (Groza kick)
Cleve—FG Groza 3

Stat Leaders

Passing
Balt—Unitas (12-20-95) 0 TDs, 2 Int, L-23
Cleve—Ryan (11-18-206) 3 TDs, 1 Int, L-51

Rushing
Balt—Moore (9-40), Hill (9-31), Unitas (6-30)
Cleve—Brown (27-114), L-46, Green (10-29)

Receiving
Balt—Berry (3-38), Orr (2-31), Lorick (3-18)
Cleve—Collins (5-130), Brown (3-37), Brewer (2-26)
ATT: 79,544.

NFL WESTERN DIVISION PLAYOFF
Dec. 26, 1965 Lambeau Field

Green Bay 13, Baltimore 10

Baltimore	7	3	0	0	0—10
Green Bay	0	0	7	3	3—13

Balt—Shinnick 25 fumble (Anderson) return (Michaels kick)
Balt—FG Michaels 15
GB—Hornung 1 run (Chandler kick)
GB—FG Chandler 22
GB—FG Chandler 25

Stat Leaders

Passing
Balt—Matte (2-12-40), 0 TDs, 0 Int, L-16
GB—Bratkowski (22-39-248), 0 Tds, 2 Int, L-33

Rushing
Balt—Matte (17-57), Hill (16-57), Moore (12-33)
GB—Taylor (23-60), Hornung (10-33), Pitts (3-14)

Receiving
Balt—Mackey (3-25), Moore (2-15)
GB—Anderson (8-78), Dowler (5-50), Hornung (4-42), Dale (3-63)
ATT: 50,484.

NFL PLAYOFF
Dec. 22, 1968 Baltimore Memorial Stadium

Baltimore 24, Minnesota 14

Minnesota	0	0	0	14—14
Baltimore	0	7	14	3—24

Balt—Mitchell 3 pass from Morrall (Michaels kick)

Balt—Mackey 49 pass from Morrall (Michaels kick)
Balt—Curtis 60 fumble return (Michaels kick)
Minn—Martin 1 pass from Kapp (Cox kick)
Balt—FG Michaels 33
Minn—Brown 7 pass from Kapp (Cox kick)

Stat Leaders

Passing
Balt—Morrall (13-22-280), 2 TDs, 1 Int, L-49
Minn—Kapp (26-44-287), 2 Tds, 2 Int

Rushing
Balt—Matte (14-31), Hill (8-10)
Minn—Kapp (10-52), Brown (10-30)

Receiving
Balt—Richardson (6-148), Mackey (3-92), Orr (2-36)
Minn—Brown (8-82), Washington (5-95), Beasley (5-69)
ATT: 60,238.

NFL CHAMPIONSHIP
Dec. 27, 1968 Cleveland Stadium

Baltimore 34, Cleveland 0

Baltimore	0	17	7	10—34
Cleveland	0	0	0	0— 0

Balt—FG Michaels 28
Balt—Matte 1 run (Michaels kick)
Balt—Matte 12 run (Michaels kick)
Balt—Matte 2 run (Michaels kick)
Balt—FG Michaels 10
Balt—T. Brown 4 run (Michaels kick)

Stat Leaders

Passing
Balt—Morrall (11-25-269) 0 TDs, 1 Int, L-38
Clev—Nelson (11-26-132) 0 TDs, 2 Int, L-22, Ryan (2-6-19)

Rushing
Balt—Matte (17-88), L-12, Hill (11-60), T. Brown (5-18)
Clev—Kelly (13-28), Harraway (6-26)

Receiving
Balt—Richardson (3-78), Mackey (2-34), Orr (2-33)
Clev—Morin (3-41), Harraway (4-40), Warfield (2-30)
ATT: 80,628.

SUPER BOWL III
Jan. 12, 1969 Miami Orange Bowl

New York Jets 16, Baltimore 7

New York (AFL)	0	7	6	3—16
Baltimore (NFL)	0	0	0	7— 7

NY—Snell 4 run (Turner kick)
NY—FG Turner 32
NY—FG Turner 30
NY—FG Turner 9
Balt—Hill 1 run (Michaels kick)

Passing

Balt—Morrall (6-17-71) 0 TDs, 3 Int, L-30
　　Unitas (11-24-110) 0 TDs, 1 Int, L-21
NY—Namath (17-28-206) 0 TD, 0 Int, L-39
　　Parilli (0-1-0)

Rushing

Balt—Matte (11-116), L-58, Hill (9-29), L-12
NY—Snell (30-121), L-12, Boozer, (10-29)

Receiving

Balt—Richardson (6-58), Orr (3-42), Mackey (3-35)
NY—Sauer (8-133), Snell (4-40)
ATT: 75,337.

AFC PLAYOFF
Dec. 26, 1970 Baltimore Memorial Stadium

Baltimore 17, Cincinnati 0

Cincinnati	0	0	0	0— 0
Baltimore	7	3	0	7—17

Balt—Jefferson 45 pass from Unitas (O'Brien kick)
Balt—FG O'Brien 44
Balt—Hinton 53 pass from Unitas (O'Brien kick)

Stat Leaders

Passing

Balt—Unitas (6-17-145), 2 TDs, 0 Int, L-53
Cin—Carter (7-20-64), 0 TDs, 1 Int, L-29
　　Wyche (1-1-29), 0 TDs, 1 Int

Rushing

Balt—Bulaich (25-116), Nowatzke (10-25)
Cin—Robinson (5-25), Phillips (10-12)

Receiving

Balt—Hinton (3-86), Jefferson (2-51)
Cin—Myers (4-66), Phillips (2-12)
ATT: 51,127.

AFC CHAMPIONSHIP
Jan. 3, 1971 Baltimore Memorial Stadium

Baltimore 27, Oakland 17

Oakland	0	3	7	7—17
Baltimore	3	7	10	7—27

Balt—FG O'Brien 16
Balt—Bulaich 2 run (O'Brien kick)
Oak—FG Blanda 48
Oak—Biletnikoff 38 pass from Blanda (Blanda kick)
Balt—FG O'Brien 23
Balt—Bulaich 11 run (O'Brien kick)
Oak—Wells 15 pass from Blanda (Blanda kick)
Balt—Perkins 68 pass from Unitas (O'Brien kick)

Passing

Balt—Unitas (11-30-245), 1 TD, 0 Int, L-68
Oak—Lamonica (1-4-6), 0 TD, 0 Int
　　Blanda (17-32-271), 2 TDs, 3 Int, L-38

Rushing

Balt—Bulaich (22-71), Nowatzke (8-32)
Oak—Dixon (10-51), C. Smith (9-44)

Receiving

Balt—Hinton (5-115), Perkins (2-80), Jefferson (3-36)
Oak—Wells (5-108), Belitnikoff (5-92)
ATT: 56,368.

SUPER BOWL V
Jan. 17, 1971 Miami Orange Bowl

Baltimore 16, Dallas 13

Baltimore (AFC)	0	6	0	10—16
Dallas (NFC)	3	10	0	0—13

Dall—FG Clark 14
Dall—FG Clark 30
Balt—Mackey 75 pass from Unitas (O'Brien kick blocked)
Dall—Thomas 7 pass from Morton (Clark kick)
Balt—Nowatzke 2 run (O'Brien kick)
Balt—FG O'Brien 32

Passing

Balt—Unitas (3-8-88), 1 TD, 2 Int, L-75
     Morrall (7-15-147), 1 Int, L-65, Havrilak (1-1-25)
Dall—Morton (12-26-127), 1 TD, 3 Int, L-41

Rushing

Balt—Nowatzke (10-33), Bulaich (18-28)
Dall—Garrison (12-65), Thomas (18-37)

Receiving

Balt—Jefferson (3-52), Mackey (2-80)
Dall—Reeves (5-46), Thomas (4-21)
ATT: 79,204.

AFC PLAYOFF
Dec. 26, 1971 Cleveland Stadium

Baltimore 20, Cleveland 3

Baltimore	0	14	3	3—20
Cleveland	0	0	3	0— 3

Balt—Nottingham 1 run (O'Brien kick)
Balt—Nottingham 7 run (O'Brien kick)
Cle—FG Cockroft 14
Balt—FG O'Brien 42
Balt—FG O'Brien 15

Stat Leaders

Passing

Balt—Unitas (13-21-143), 0 TDs, 1 Int, L-26
Cle—Nelsen (9-21-104), 0 TDs, 3 Int, L-39
     Phipps (3-6-27), 0 TDs, 0 Int, L-13

Rushing

Balt—Nottingham (23-92), Matte (16-26)
Cle—Kelly (14-49), Scott (8-25)

Receiving
Balt—Mitchell (5-73), Matte (3-22), Hinton (2-30)
Cle—Scott (5-41), Kelly (4-24)
ATT: 74,082.

AFC CHAMPIONSHIP
Jan. 2, 1972 Miami Orange Bowl

Miami 21, Baltimore 0

Baltimore	0	0	0	0— 0
Miami	7	0	7	7—21

Mia—Warfield 75 pass from Griese (Yepremian kick)
Mia—Anderson 62 interception return (Yepremian kick)
Mia—Csonka 5 run (Yepremian kick)

Passing
Balt—Unitas (20-36-224) 0 TDs, 3 Int, L-27
Mia—Griese (4-8-158) 1 TD, 1 Int, L-75

Rushing
Balt—McCauley (15-50), Nottingham (11-33)
Mia—Kiick (18-66), Csonka (15-63)

Receiving
Balt—Hinton (6-98), Nottingham (4-26)
Mia—Warfield (2-125), Twilley (2-33)
ATT: 75,629.

AFC PLAYOFF
Dec. 27, 1975 Three Rivers Stadium

Pittsburgh 28, Baltimore 10

Baltimore	0	7	3	0—10
Pittsburgh	7	0	7	14—28

Pitt—Harris 8 run (Gerela kick)
Balt—Doughty 5 pass from Domres (Linhart kick)
Balt—Linhart 21 FG
Pitt—Bleier 7 run (Gerela kick)
Pitt—Bradshaw 2 run (Gerela kick)
Pitt—Russell 93 fumble return (Gerela kick)

Stat Leaders

Passing
Balt—Jones (11-6-91), 0 TD, 0 Int, L-58
Pitt—Bradshaw (13-8-103), 0 TD, 2 Int, L-34

Rushing
Balt—Mitchell (26-63), Domres (4-17)
Pitt—Harris (27-153), Bleier (12-28)

Receiving
Balt—Mitchell (4-20), Doughty (2-63-1)
Pitt—Lewis (3-65), Swann (2-15), Bleier (2-14)
ATT: 49,053.

AFC PLAYOFF
Dec. 19, 1976 Baltimore Memorial Stadium

Pittsburgh 40, Baltimore 14

Pittsburgh	9	17	0	14—40
Baltimore	7	0	0	7—14

Pitt—Lewis 76 pass from Bradshaw (kick failed) (1:39, 1Q)
Pitt—Gerela 45 FG (8:30, 1Q)
Balt—Carr 17 pass from Jones (Linhart kick) (14:43, 1Q)
Pitt—Harrison 1 run (Gerela kick) (1:57, 2Q)
Pitt—Swann 29 pass from Bradshaw (Gerela kick) (14:07 2Q)
Pitt—Gerela 25 FG (14:56 2Q)
Pitt—Swann 11 pass from Bradshaw (Gerela kick) (0:50 4Q)
Balt—Leaks 1 run (Linhart kick) (4:16 4Q)
Pitt—Harrison 10 run (Mansfield kick) (7:23, 4Q)

Stat Leaders

Passing
Pitt—Bradshaw (18-14-264), 3 TD, 0 Int, L-76; Kruczek (6-5-44), 0 TD, 0 Int, L-15
Balt—Jones (25-11-144), 1 TD, 2 Int, L-25

Rushing
Pitt—Harris (18-132), Harrison (10-40-2), Fuqua (11-54)
Balt—Mitchell (16-55), Leaks (4-12-1)

Receiving
Pitt—Lewis (2-103-1), Swann (5-77-2), Harris (3-24), Harrison (4-37), Fuqua (2-34), Bell (2-25)
Balt—Mitchell (5-42), Chester (3-42), Carr (2-35-1)
ATT: 60,020.